CUISINE ECONOMIQUE

ALSO BY JACQUES PEPIN

The Other Half of the Egg (1975)
Jacques Pépin: A French Chef Cooks at Home (1975)
La Technique (1976)
La Méthode (1979)
Everyday Cooking with Jacques Pépin (1982)
The Art of Cooking, Volumes 1 and 2 (1987/1988)
A Fare for the Heart (1988)
A Fare That Fits (1989)
The Short-Cut Cook (1990)
Today's Gourmet (1991)

Cuisine Économique

Jacques Pepin

WILLIAM MORROW AND COMPANY, INC.   NEW YORK

LIBRARY OF CONGRESS CATALOGING-IN-
PUBLICATION DATA
PEPIN, JACQUES.
CUISINE ECONOMIQUE / JACQUES PEPIN.
P.   CM.
INCLUDES INDEX.
ISBN 0-688-11145-9
1. COOKERY. I. TITLE.
TX714.P45   1992
641.5-DC20   91-27017
                                        CIP

PRINTED IN THE UNITED STATES OF AMERICA

FIRST EDITION

1   2   3   4   5   6   7   8   9   10

BOOK DESIGN BY RICHARD ORIOLO

*To Norma Galehouse
with my gratitude for her
hard work and dedication*

CONTENTS

INTRODUCTION

All good cooks share a profound respect for raw ingredients, a sound, commonsense approach to their trade, and a thorough knowledge of the cooking process. When cooks really understand the mechanics of a recipe and the true nature of each ingredient, they handle the food with proper consideration, using it in the most functional way possible and in its entirety, one way or another. These principles of kitchen economics apply to great cooks everywhere, whether they be Chinese, Italian, German, French, or American.

As I travel around the country and work with young chefs, I am always more impressed with those who produce good, well-cooked food with speed, organization, cleanliness, and economy than those who create complicated "food art" at the expense of thrift, order, and taste. Economy, not only of food but also of time and money, reflects the cook's comprehension and intelligence about his craft. Uncontrived economy is standard practice in a good kitchen. Like a well-choreographed ballet, there is a natural flow in this style of cooking, where no motion is wasted, no ingredient discarded.

Because I was born into a family of restaurateurs and have worked all my life in a kitchen, it is second nature for me to be thrifty. To save time, for example, I reuse a pot several times in a logical sequence—cooking foods that are nonsticky before those that stick and stain—before washing it. Likewise with a food processor—I process the dry ingredients before the wet ones, so the processor needs to be washed only once. And I always save the trimmings of meats and vegetables for a stock, soup, or eventually, a sauce.

Throughout *Cuisine Economique* I make use of inexpensive cuts of meat and economical poultry (see Lamb Navarin, page 58, Spicy Grilled Beef Roast, page 125, Fiery Chili with Red Beans, page 178, Veal Tendrons and Tarragon Sauce, page 228, Braised Pork Roast with Sweet Potatoes, page 173, and Fricassee of Dark Turkey Meat, page 12.) But though economy is a primary concern in my meat selections, it is never at the expense of flavor. Many of the dishes in this book are updated versions of the favorite meals of my childhood in postwar France. Food and money were in short supply then, and nothing was more welcome on a Sunday afternoon than a stuffed veal breast roasted to succulent tenderness and served with its pan juices and potatoes (see Stuffed Roast Veal Breast with Potatoes, page 62). I enjoy these low-cost dishes as much today as I did then, and I treasure the happy memories they evoke.

Buying seasonally is another way to approach economy in the kitchen, and so I've arranged all the recipes in this book into seasonal menus. More often than not, I create my menus at the supermarket, looking for the best, but also the least expensive, and striking a balance betweeen the two.

I buy fruits and vegetables when they are most flavorful and least expensive—in season. And I apply this same rule of economy to my other food purchases as well: I buy whole turkeys for a variety of preparations when they are most attractively priced, in the fall and winter; I plan lamb and ham main dishes in the spring, when there are often specials on these meats. Shellfish and fish are usually expensive, so I purchase more seafood (mackerel, bluefish, blackfish, and shellfish) in the summer, when its's available for less because it's more abundant. I also know that first impressions are not everything: For example, the outside leaves of a head of escarole may be wilted or damaged but I will still buy it because the center, the part I want to use, is white, firm, sweet, and tender. Or I may not have any intention of serving expensive artichokes on my menu. Yet if the leftover rack offers artichokes with yellowish and brownish leaves at a bargain price, I buy them because I know they will be ideal for artichoke bottoms.

By the way, you won't find many desserts in these menus, and when they are offered, they're generally simple fruit concoctions (see Cranberry

Kisel, page 187, Apple Stew, page 224, and Honeyed Melon, page 94). In this thrift-conscious, health-oriented age, I view desserts as a frill, something to omit entirely day-to-day or replace with a piece of fresh fruit as a light finish to a family meal. Good home cooking should be focused on main dishes, and special desserts (see Choux à la Crème, page 59) should be something extra you enjoy when guests join you for dinner.

Whenever possible, I buy the exact quantities of the ingredients I need, to eliminate creating leftovers that might spoil. However, when you do have them, leftovers can be great resources. Unfortunately, in our society, the word *leftover* has a derogatory meaning, implying food that is cheap, dried out, reheated, and of a lesser quality.

A good cook is never apologetic about leftovers. The common mistake is to try to re-serve them in their original form. A roasted chicken is good only when fresh. Reheated, it tastes like a leftover, with all the word's pejorative connotations. But if the cooked chicken is served in a hash or in a cream sauce, or is transformed into a salad, it will taste as it should—like a freshly made dish.

The proof of the pudding is in the eating, of course, but if the result of this style of cooking is high-quality food in minimal time and with minimal effort and money, you can be sure that a great cook is behind the stove. And he's practicing *cuisine économique.* What follows is a perfect example of this philosophy at work.

A MASTER LESSON IN ECONOMY: TURKEY

MENU 1.

Turkey Stock Soup with Lettuce Strips
Scaloppine of White Turkey Meat
Escarole Salad with Turkey Crackling
Pear Tatin

MENU 2.

Turkey Liver Toasts
Fricassee of Dark Turkey Meat
Pear Tatin

When a great cook approaches a whole bird such as a chicken or turkey, or a whole lamb, he or she thinks about how to make something from each part of the animal without wasting a scrap. Trimmed meat is set aside, the trimmings are turned into ground meat, and the bones go into stock, which will eventually become a sauce.

In the recipes that follow, I demonstrate how turkey lends itself to an almost unlimited number of dishes, far beyond what appears on the Thanksgiving table. These recipes can be prepared, of course, with turkey parts—legs, breasts, wings, necks, and livers—all of which are available prepackaged at most supermarkets. In the fall and winter, however, near holiday times (and at other times of the year when your market does special promotions), it is less expensive to buy a whole bird, bone it, and use the various parts in a number of recipes than it is to buy the parts separately. Some of these dishes can be enjoyed one day, and others consumed over the next few days. Parts of the turkey can also be frozen for use at a later date in other recipes (see Grilled Turkey Wings, page 119).

Starting with a fifteen-pound turkey, separate the two legs from the carcass first, and then remove the wings at the joint of the shoulder by prying your knife into the joint with one hand while pulling on the wing with the other. Next remove the two breasts, following the carcass bone with your knife while you pull gently on the breast pieces to free them.

I use the bones as the base of a creamy soup made with a chiffonade of lettuce. I brown the legs and wings and combine with herbs in a fricassee of dark meat with brown rice. The breast meat is sliced and pounded thin for scaloppine with shiitake mushrooms and Cognac sauce, and the skin baked until very crisp, broken into pieces, and sprinkled on an escarole salad. The liver is cooked, chopped and spooned on toast as a stylish hors d'oeuvre. (For the recipe that follows on page 11, I added some additional livers, available prepackaged at the supermarket, to make a more generous amount of this quick and easy hors d'oeuvre.)

Clearly the turkey is endlessly versatile. The fricassee, for instance, is an earthy, one-dish meal; the scaloppine is elegant and rich. These recipes are all made with turkey, but other poultry could be used instead.

Moreover, many other recipes could be made with the turkey parts. For example, the bones could be used to make stock—brown as well as white—rather than soup. Then the stock could be made into sauces. The dark meat could be blended in a wine-flavored stew, and the wings could be braised with dried beans or split peas. The legs could be boned out and tied to make a roast, as could the whole breast. The turkey meat could be ground and made into a mousse, a pâté, or dumplings. And, if the notion of economy is understood and applied, whatever vegetables you have in the refrigerator could be substituted for those in the recipes. A flexible approach to cooking—one that allows for changes, whether they are motivated by whim or necessity—is far more economical than a strict adherence to recipes.

I have created two menus from the various turkey recipes that follow, although you can devise your own menu(s) based on a different combination of these dishes. Both of my menus feature the same beautiful and flavorful dessert, Pear Tatin.

TURKEY STOCK SOUP WITH LETTUCE STRIPS

FOR THE STOCK

3 *pounds turkey carcass (including back and neck) (approximate yield from a 15-pound turkey)*

1 *teaspoon dried thyme*

2 *bay leaves*

1/2 *teaspoon crushed peppercorns*

3 *tablespoons unsalted butter*

1 *cup coarsely chopped onion*

1 *cup coarsely chopped leeks*

1 *pound peeled potatoes, cut into 1-inch cubes*

1 *teaspoon salt*

FOR THE GARNISH

1 *medium-size head Boston lettuce (about 5 ounces)*

2 *tablespoons unsalted butter*

TOTAL TIME:
4 HOURS

1. *For the stock:* Place the bones in a large pot, cover with 12 cups water, and bring to a boil. Skim off and discard foam that rises to the surface. Add the thyme, bay leaves, and peppercorns. Boil gently for 3 hours.

2. Strain to remove the bones and measure the stock. You should have about 8 cups. Boil to reduce the stock to 8 cups if you have more; if you have less, add enough water to attain this yield.

3. Melt the butter in a stockpot. Add the onion and leeks and sauté over medium heat for 2 minutes. Add the 8 cups stock, the potatoes, and salt. Bring to a boil and boil gently, partially covered, for 45 minutes.

continued

4. Strain the soup, reserving the liquid, and process the solids in a food processor until very smooth. Combine with the reserved liquid. (If the solids are processed with the liquid, the mixture tends to be too foamy.)

5. *Meanwhile, for the garnish:* Separate the lettuce into leaves and wash them thoroughly. Pile the leaves together and cut them crosswise into thin strips (chiffonnade). Melt the butter in a stainless steel saucepan and add the lettuce. Cook for 1 to 2 minutes, until wilted.

6. At serving time, combine the garnish with the soup. The soup can be served hot or cold.

YIELD: 8 SERVINGS

SCALOPPINE OF WHITE TURKEY MEAT

TOTAL TIME:
15 TO 20 MINUTES
PLUS MUSHROOM
SOAKING TIME

2 *ounces dried shiitake mushrooms, soaked in 3 cups lukewarm water for 1 hour*

6 *tablespoons unsalted butter*

1$^{1}/_{2}$ *teaspoons salt, or more to taste*

4$^{1}/_{2}$ *pounds cleaned turkey breast meat (yield from 1 15-pound turkey), cut into 12 large cutlets, about 6 ounces each, and pounded until about $^{3}/_{8}$ inch thick*

1 *teaspoon freshly ground black pepper, or more to taste*

6 *scallions, chopped (about $^{1}/_{2}$ cup)*

3 *cloves garlic, peeled, crushed, and chopped (about 1 tablespoon)*

2 *tablespoons Cognac*

1$^{1}/_{2}$ *cups heavy cream*

1 *teaspoon potato starch dissolved in 1 tablespoon water (optional)*

A few drops lemon juice

1 *tablespoon chopped chives, for garnish*

1. Drain the shiitake mushrooms, reserving the juice, and remove the stems, which are fibrous. (You can add them to the stock for the Turkey Stock Soup with Lettuce Strips.)

2. Cut the caps into ¹/₂-inch strips. Strain the juice through paper towels and reduce it over high heat to 1 cup. Set aside.

3. At serving time, divide the butter between two large saucepans or three skillets. Place the pans over medium heat and when the butter is hot, add the turkey in one layer. Sprinkle it with the salt and pepper and cook it over medium to high heat for approximately 1 minute on each side. Arrange in an ovenproof dish and set in a 180-degree oven to keep warm.

4. Add the scallions and garlic to the saucepans and sauté for 30 seconds. Add the Cognac and ignite it, taking care to protect yourself from the flame. Add the reduced mushroom juices and cream and bring to a boil, stirring to dissolve and mix in any solidified juices. Add any juices that have collected around the turkey to the sauce, and then strain the sauce into a clean saucepan. Add the mushroom strips. Bring to a boil and simmer for 3 minutes. Add salt and pepper to taste and add the dissolved potato starch if the mixture needs thickening. Stir in the lemon juice.

5. Arrange the scaloppine on a platter and coat them with the sauce and mushrooms. Sprinkle with the chives, and serve immediately.

YIELD: 8 SERVINGS

ESCAROLE SALAD WITH TURKEY CRACKLING

TOTAL TIME:
ABOUT 45
MINUTES

Skin from 1 15-pound turkey (about 1 pound)

Salt to taste

1 *large or 2 smaller heads escarole (choose heads with the whitest possible insides, indicating the nuttiest flavor; the green leaves tend to be tough and bitter)*

FOR THE DRESSING

2 *teaspoons Dijon-style mustard*

1 TO 2 *cloves garlic, peeled, crushed, and finely chopped (about 1 teaspoon)*

1 *tablespoon red wine vinegar*

$1/2$ *teaspoon freshly ground black pepper*

$1/4$ *teaspoon salt*

$1/3$ *cup oil (half olive and half canola, or a mixture of olive, canola, and safflower oil—or $1/4$ cup of one of these oils and 2 tablespoons of the fat rendered by cooking the turkey skin)*

1. To remove the skin from the turkey, cut along the backbone with a sharp knife and begin to pull on the skin to help separate it from the carcass. Continue pulling and cutting until the entire skin is removed from the carcass. Do not worry if you make holes in the skin or if you cut it into smaller pieces.

2. To make the crackling, spread the turkey skin on a large cookie sheet in one layer, stretching it out thin in one large or several smaller pieces. Sprinkle with salt and bake in a preheated 400-degree oven for about 30 minutes, until crisp and brown all over. The skin will have shrunk considerably. Cool slightly and lift from the surrounding fat. Break into $1/2$-inch pieces and set aside. You should have 1 to $1 1/2$ cups of crackling. Reserve the fat in the pan for sautéeing vegetables or for adding to the vinaigrette.

3. Trim off and discard any outside escarole leaves that are very green or damaged and cut the remaining leaves into 2-inch pieces. Wash thoroughly, lifting the leaves up out of the water. Dry well in a salad spinner. You should have approximately 9 to 10 cups of washed escarole.

4. *For the dressing:* Stir together the mustard, garlic, vinegar, pepper and salt in a bowl. Add the oil and/or turkey fat slowly and mix well. (The dressing should be slightly separated, not homogenized, so the greens are shiny when tossed with the dressing.)

5. At serving time, add the dressing to the greens and toss well. Sprinkle with the crackling and serve immediately.

YIELD: 8 SERVINGS

PEAR TATIN

The original *tarte tatin* was an upside-down apple tart created years ago by the two Tatin sisters in Lamotte Beuvon, France. I replace the apples with pears in the following recipe and add almonds and raisins for a sophisticated result.

FOR THE CARAMEL

$^1/_4$ *cup sugar*

3 *tablespoons water*

3 *Bosc pears (about 1 $^1/_2$ pounds)*

2 *tablespoons unsalted butter*

$^2/_3$ *cups water*

2 *tablespoons sliced almonds*

2 *tablespoons golden raisins*

FOR THE DOUGH

$^1/_2$ *cup all-purpose flour*

2 *tablespoons unsalted butter*

2 *teaspoons sugar*

1$^1/_2$ *tablespoons milk*

1. *For the caramel:* Place the $^1/_4$ cup sugar and the 3 tablespoons water in an ovenproof 10-inch skillet. Cook over medium to high heat for about 5 minutes, until the mixture turns a light caramel color. Remove from the heat and swirl the caramel in the skillet to cool and harden it. (If the caramel darkens too much as it continues to cook in the pan's residual heat, plunge the base of the skillet in cool water to stop the cooking.)

continued

2. Peel the pears, cut them in half lengthwise, and core them. Arrange the pear halves, cut side up, on the caramel so the pointed ends of the pears meet in the center. Add the 2 tablespoons butter and the $\frac{2}{3}$ cup water. Bring to a boil (the caramel will melt). Cover the skillet with a lid, reduce the heat to low, and cook gently for about 20 minutes, checking occasionally, until all the water has evaporated and the mixture in the pan has caramelized again. (By then, the pears should be partially cooked.)

3. *Meanwhile, for the dough*: In the bowl of a food processor place the flour, the 2 tablespoons butter, and the sugar. Process for about 10 seconds. Add the milk and process for another 10 seconds. Transfer the unformed dough onto a sheet of plastic wrap and press on it until it forms a cohesive ball. Place another piece of plastic wrap on top of the dough and roll it with a rolling pin between the two plastic sheets to create a circle about the diameter of your skillet (10 inches). Refrigerate the dough (still encased in plastic) to firm it slightly.

4. After the pears have cooked for 20 minutes, fill their hollow centers with the almonds and raisins. Remove the dough from the refrigerator, peel off the top sheet of plastic wrap, and invert the dough on top of the pears. Peel off the remaining plastic sheet. Place the skillet in a preheated 400-degree oven for about 30 minutes. (By then, the dough should be nicely browned on top and, when you tilt the pan, there should be a rich layer of caramel in the bottom.) Set the skillet aside until serving time.

5. If the pear tatin has cooled beyond lukewarm at serving time, rewarm it on top of the stove until the caramel is soft again (the whole mixture will move in the pan when you shake it). Not more than $\frac{1}{2}$ hour before serving, invert a serving plate on top of the dough and turn the warm tart out onto the plate. Slice into portions, serving half a pear per person, and serve.

YIELD: 6 SERVING

TURKEY LIVER TOASTS

2 *tablespoons unsalted butter*

1 *tablespoon virgin olive oil*

6 TO 8 *turkey livers, halved and the sinew trimmed from the center (see Note)*

Salt and freshly ground black pepper to taste

1 TO 2 *cloves garlic, peeled, crushed, and finely chopped (about 1 teaspoon)*

2 *tablespoons chopped parsley or chives or a mixture of both*

40 *thin slices of bread from a baguette about 1 1/2 inches in diameter, toasted under the broiler*

TOTAL TIME:
10 MINUTES

1. Heat the butter and oil in one very large or two smaller skillets. Sprinkle the livers with salt and freshly ground pepper. When the oil and butter begin to smoke, add the livers (being careful of splattering) in one layer and cook for approximately 1 to 1 1/2 minutes on each side. The livers should remain pink inside. Stir in the chopped garlic and herbs and immediately remove the pan from the heat. Transfer the livers to a plate.

2. Arrange the toasts on a large platter. Cut each turkey liver half into 3 or 4 pieces. Arrange the liver pieces on the toasts and serve immediately.

NOTE: If turkey livers are not available at your market, substitute chicken livers, using about a dozen to replace the 6 to 8 turkey livers. Cut each cooked halved chicken liver in half again to serve on the toasts.

YIELD: 40 TOASTS, 8 SERVINGS

FRICASSEE OF DARK TURKEY MEAT

TOTAL TIME:
2 HOURS AND
10 MINUTES

3 *tablespoons unsalted butter*

2 *turkey legs plus the 2 wings from 1 15-pound turkey (about 5 pounds total), each wing (tip removed) halved at the joint and each leg cut into 5 pieces, 2 from the drumstick and 3 from the thigh (14 pieces altogether)*

3 *cups diced (1-inch) onions*

5 *cloves garlic, peeled, crushed, and chopped (about 2 tablespoons)*

1 *piece fresh ginger, peeled and finely chopped (about 2 tablespoons)*

1 *teaspoon cumin powder*

1/2 *teaspoon red pepper flakes*

2 *bay leaves*

2 *teaspoons salt*

1 *teaspoon freshly ground black pepper*

1 1/2 *cups brown rice*

1 *cup dried tomatoes, cut into 1-inch pieces*

1 *cup tiny fresh peas, blanched briefly in boiling water*

1. Melt the butter in a large Dutch oven or stockpot (preferably heavy aluminum, cast-iron, or copper) and add half the pieces of turkey in one layer. Brown, turning occasionally, over medium to high heat for 15 to 20 minutes, then transfer to a tray. Add the remaining turkey pieces to the skillet and brown them as before. Remove the turkey from the pot and set it aside on the tray with the other browned turkey.

2. Add the onions to the pot and sauté them over medium heat for 10 minutes. Return the turkey to the pot, add 3 cups water and all the remaining ingredients except for the peas, and stir well. Bring to a boil, stirring. Cover, reduce the heat to low, and cook gently for 70 minutes, adding up to 2 cups more water, if necessary, until all the liquid has been absorbed by the rice and the rice and meat are tender. At this point, some or all of the bones can be removed, if desired.

3. Mix in the peas and serve immediately.

YIELD: 8 SERVINGS

Spring

A SIMPLE COUNTRY DINNER

Garlic Soup
Cayettes with Spinach
Skillet-Roasted Potatoes with Rosemary

HARBINGERS OF SPRING

Asparagus au Beurre
Mussels Chinoise
Rice with Onions

HOT CURRY WITH COOL FRUITS

Cheese and Tomato Salad

ONE CHICKEN, TWO DISHES

Chicken Diable
Cauliflower and Crumbs

Lentil and Chicken Fricassee

SENTIMENTAL FAVORITES

Vegetable and Oatmeal Soup
Sausage and Potato Ragout
Escarole Salad

SALUTE TO SPRING

Garlicky Romanine with Croutons
Red Beans and Pork
Yellow Rice with Achiote
Guava with Cream Cheese and Mint

SUNDAY SUPPER

Gratin of Eggs and Spinach ·
Lamb Navarin
Choux à la Crème

A TRENCHERMAN'S DELIGHT

Stuffed Roast Veal Breast with Potatoes
Napa Cabbage Salad
Banana Ice Cream with Rum

A SIMPLE COUNTRY DINNER

Garlic Soup
Cayettes with Spinach
Skillet-Roasted Potatoes with Rosemary

Traveling around the country thirty-some weeks a year to teach cooking classes, I eat often in restaurants, some great, some not so great. Occasionally, my stomach rebels against my excesses and I long for some plain, unadorned vegetable soup, like the garlic soup that follows.

Don't be alarmed by the fact that this soup contains fifteen cloves of garlic. Granted, that much would be prohibitively strong if it were only lightly sautéed for a dish or used raw in a salad. But cooked as it is here with potatoes and stock, it becomes surprisingly mild in flavor, without the powerful odor or taste characteristic of raw garlic. Be sure to discard the stem ends and any damaged sections of the peeled cloves before cooking them.

Cayettes with Spinach is an excellent follow-up to this earthy soup. *Cayettes* is the name used in some parts of France for patties of ground meat flavored with onion and garlic and combined with greens like spinach, lettuce, Swiss chard (the most common choice in the Lyon area where I grew up), or kale, or even a mixture of these greens. Traditionally, these patties are wrapped in caul fat (a step that I have omitted) before being baked or grilled. The ground meat used for cayettes can be either beef or pork or a mixture of the two. I use both, and add some chicken livers as well.

With this earthy menu, I would serve a robust wine, such as a red Zinfandel. Dried fruits and nuts (raisins, apricots, walnuts) make a good finish to this cool-weather country dinner.

GARLIC SOUP

TOTAL TIME: ABOUT 1 HOUR

There are almost endless possibilities for variation here. Potatoes are my favorite thickening agent for garlic soup, but it can also be thickened with a roux of flour and butter or with bread, the traditional choice in the south of France, where this dish is a specialty. Onions and scallions can be used instead of leeks, although the soup won't have the same subtle and delicate taste. If you do use leeks, include as much of the green leaves as possible for flavor and color.

A poultry or meat stock gives the soup more body and flavor, although it's good made with water. I purposely kept the soup simple, natural, and low in calories, but for a special party you could enrich it by adding a cup of heavy or light cream at the last minute.

And finally, for the croutons, instead of sautéing cubes of white bread, you could cut thin slices from a small French baguette or a large country-style loaf, oil them lightly, and bake them in a 400-degree oven until brown and crisp.

2 *medium-size leeks*

¼ *cup canola or safflower oil*

12 TO 15 *cloves garlic (½ to ¾ cup), peeled and stems and any damaged parts removed and discarded*

7 *cups homemade chicken stock or canned chicken broth*

6 TO 8 *potatoes (about 2 pounds), peeled and cut into 1-inch cubes (about 4 cups)*

1 *teaspoon salt, or to taste*

4 *slices firm-textured white bread, cut into ½-inch cubes (about 1½ cups)*

2 *tablespoons unsalted butter*

1. Trim the leeks, removing and discarding only the roots, fibrous tips, and damaged outer leaves. Slice, rinse thoroughly, and pat dry with paper towels. You should have about 2 cups.

2. Heat 2 tablespoons of the oil in a heavy pot. When hot, add the leeks and garlic. Cook over medium heat for about 3 minutes, until the vegetables begin to soften. Add the stock, potatoes, and salt, and bring to a boil. Cover, reduce the heat, and boil gently for 30 minutes.

3. While the soup is cooking, make the croutons: Heat the remaining 2 tablespoons oil in a large skillet. When hot, sauté the bread cubes, stirring almost continuously, until they are browned evenly on all sides. Remove with a slotted spoon and drain on paper towels.

4. When the soup mixture is cooked, push it through a food mill or puree it in a food processor. To puree in a food processor, first strain the soup through a fine sieve. Place the solids in the bowl of the processor and process until smooth, then combine with the reserved liquid. (If the solids are processed with too much liquid, the mixture becomes foamy, yielding a soup with a frothy texture like baby food.)

5. Stir the butter into the hot soup and serve with the croutons.

YIELD: 6 TO 8 SERVINGS (7 TO 8 CUPS)

Cayettes with Spinach

TOTAL TIME:
ABOUT 1 HOUR

The cayettes can be prepared and even cooked ahead. Serve them hot or cold, and pass hot mustard at the table. Excellent with a green salad dressed with a garlicky vinaigrette, they are also wonderful with pasta, beans, mashed or hash brown potatoes, or with Skillet-Roasted Potatoes with Rosemary (page 20).

10 *ounces (about 10 cups) washed spinach (or a mixture of spinach, Swiss chard, kale, and salad greens)*

2 *tablespoons olive oil*

1 *large onion (about 6 ounces), peeled and chopped (about 1 cup)*

8 *scallions, cleaned and chopped into ¹/₂-inch pieces (about ³/₄ cup)*

3 *large cloves garlic, peeled, crushed, and chopped (about 1 tablespoon)*

5 *chicken livers (about 5 ounces total)*

1 *pound ground beef*

¹/₂ *pound ground pork*

1 *teaspoon salt*

¹/₂ *teaspoon freshly ground black pepper*

¹/₄ *teaspoon grated nutmeg*

1 *tablespoon vegetable oil*

1. Stack the spinach leaves one on top of another and cut them into 1-inch-wide strips.

2. Heat the olive oil in a skillet. When hot, add the onion and scallions and cook for about 1 to 1¹/₂ minutes, until the vegetables are softened but not brown. Add the garlic, stir well, then add the spinach. Sauté, stirring, for about 2 minutes, until the spinach has wilted but is still bright green. Set aside to cool.

3. Place the chicken livers in the bowl of a food processor and process for about 10 seconds, until pureed. Add the ground beef and pork and process for 5 to 10 seconds, just until mixed. Set aside.

4. When the spinach mixture is cool, mix well with the ground meat. Add the salt, pepper, and nutmeg and mix well.

5. Grease a roasting pan with the vegetable oil. Wet your hands under cold water and form large spoonfuls of the meat-vegetable mixture into 12 equal-size patties. Arrange the patties close together in the roasting pan and bake in a preheated 375-degree oven for 25 minutes. Serve two cayettes per person.

YIELD: 6 SERVINGS

*S*PECIAL TIP: *The cayettes are very good cold—so good, in fact, that instead of eating two of them each for dinner, members of my family usually elect to save one of theirs to enjoy cold the following day. To serve the cayettes cold, slice them (they will have a nice pink interior) and arrange them on a bed of salad greens. Sprinkle with vinegar and olive oil, if you like, and garnish with sliced tomatoes. Pass some Dijon-style mustard and serve with a good French bread.*

Skillet-Roasted Potatoes with Rosemary

TOTAL TIME:

25 MINUTES

Although the ingredients for this dish can be assembled ahead in the pan, for best results don't cook the potatoes until just before serving.

You can grow rosemary indoors in pots the year round, although it is available fresh at many supermarkets throughout the year and at farm markets in the summer. If you can't find it fresh, substitute dried rosemary leaves.

2 *pounds small new potatoes (about 24), thoroughly washed and any damaged spots removed*

3 *tablespoons olive oil*

1 *tablespoon unsalted butter*

1 *cup water*

$\frac{1}{4}$ *teaspoon salt*

2 *tablespoons fresh rosemary leaves or 2 teaspoons dried rosemary*

1. Place the potatoes in one layer in a large saucepan and add the oil, butter, water, and salt. Bring to a boil, cover, and cook over high heat for about 8 minutes, until the water has evaporated. Reduce the heat and continue cooking, covered, over low heat for about 10 minutes. Add the rosemary and cook, stirring occasionally, for 2 to 3 minutes longer.

2. Place the potatoes in a bowl and serve with the cayettes.

YIELD: 6 SERVINGS

HARBINGERS OF SPRING

Asparagus au Beurre
Mussels Chinoise
Rice with Onions

Spring always brings to mind young vegetables, particularly asparagus. When I was a child, my brother and I used to pick wild asparagus, which grew next to the Rhône river in Lyon.

We were partial to the pungent, somewhat bitter "butcher's broom" type, as well as asparagus acutifolius, which is very tiny and aromatic, with a stronger taste than cultivated asparagus.

Even though both green and white asparagus are cultivated in France, the white is more common there, while the green is more popular in the United States. White asparagus is slightly bitter and must be cooked longer than green asparagus, or it will be fibrous.

Green asparagus is my favorite, and I prefer large stalks with tight heads that resemble the buds of flowers. It is a fallacy that thin asparagus is younger; the vegetable emerges from the ground with a certain thickness and continues to grow upward rather than getting fatter.

Many people eat only the tender upper half of the stalks. But if the tough outer skin is removed from the lower half with a vegetable peeler, the entire spear is edible. Doubling the yield makes it well worth taking a few minutes to peel the spears.

Mussels also signal spring to me. When I first moved to Connecticut fifteen years ago, I used to go mussel hunting each spring along the coast, where they are plentiful. Unfortunately, because of pollution, I rarely pick up wild mussels anymore, relying instead on fishmongers who sell them from beds that are monitored and tested regularly for pollution.

In this menu, the mussels have an Oriental flavor. The seasonings include hot chili sauce, oyster sauce, coriander (cilantro or Chinese parsley), and garlic, producing a spicy, flavorful stock. The rice served with the mussels is a long-grain variety that cooks in chicken stock flavored with onions.

For dessert, in the spirit of spring, try strawberries sprinkled with a little sugar. And for your wine choice, I recommend a clean-tasting Italian white Orvieto.

ASPARAGUS AU BEURRE

A low-calorie vegetable, asparagus is delicious when lightly steamed, as it is here. It is best when cooked in just enough water to steam it, and it is ready—tender but still a bit firm to the bite—after only a few minutes. It makes a great first course, although it can be served as a vegetable side dish with meat, poultry, fish, or shellfish.

TOTAL TIME:
30 MINUTES

2 *dozen large asparagus stalks with tight, firm tips (about 1 1/2 pounds)*

6 *tablespoons unsalted butter*

1/2 *teaspoon salt*

3/4 *teaspoon freshly ground black pepper*

2 *tablespoons finely chopped parsley, for garnish*

1. Peel the lower half (root end) of the asparagus stalks with a vegetable peeler.

2. Bring 1/2 cup water to a boil in a large stainless steel saucepan. Add the asparagus in one layer, cover, and cook over high heat for approximately 6 minutes, to the desired tenderness. Lift the asparagus from the water (most of which will have evaporated) and arrange it on a platter.

3. Meanwhile, heat the butter in a skillet until it turns a light brown color and stops smoking.

4. Sprinkle the asparagus with the salt and pepper, and pour the hot butter over it. Garnish with the parsley, and serve immediately.

YIELD: 6 SERVINGS

MUSSELS CHINOISE

TOTAL TIME:
20 MINUTES

Of the many different types, I prefer the medium-size blue-black mussels that are heavy—indicating fullness—better than the large ones. Inexpensive and available nationwide almost year-round, mussels have a tangy, sweet taste that produces one of the best shellfish stocks. The meat is very nutritious, high in protein, low in fat, and rich in vitamins (especially A) and minerals.

6 *pounds mussels (about 14 to the pound) (see Special Tip)*

1 *medium-size onion (about 6 ounces), peeled and coarsely chopped (about 1 1/2 cups)*

3 *ripe tomatoes (about 1 pound), cut in half, seeds and juice pressed out, and flesh cut into 1/2-inch cubes (about 3 cups)*

1 1/2 *tablespoons Chinese oyster sauce*

1 *tablespoon hot Chinese chili sauce (or more or less, depending on your tolerance for spicy food)*

1 1/2 *tablespoons dark sesame oil*

1 1/2 *tablespoons canola oil*

1/2 *cup coarsely chopped coriander (cilantro leaves or Chinese parsley)*

6 *cloves garlic, peeled, crushed, and chopped (about 1 1/2 tablespoons)*

1. Remove and discard the beards from the mussels and wash them thoroughly at least twice under cool water, rubbing them against one another to help dislodge any sand.

2. Place the mussels in a large stainless steel stockpot with the remainder of the ingredients. Bring to a boil over high heat, stir well, cover, reduce the heat to low, and cook for 7 to 8 minutes, stirring occasionally, until all of the shells have opened.

3. Divide the mussels among six plates and spoon some of the pot juices over them. Serve immediately.

YIELD: 6 SERVINGS

PECIAL TIP: *If you bring mussels home from the store in a plastic bag, remove them from the bag, but do not put them in water. They need to breathe, and are best stored in the refrigerator, either in a bowl loosely covered with plastic wrap, or in a brown paper bag.*

If you find any open mussels, touch the inside gently with a knife; if the shells close, the mussels are still alive. More than anything else, rely on your nose: If an open mussel has an unpleasant odor, discard it.

RICE WITH ONIONS

TOTAL TIME:
30 MINUTES
Chances are you have all the ingredients on hand for this classic dish, which is good with most poultry, meat, or fish. Quick and easy, it rounds out this eclectic menu.

1 *tablespoon unsalted butter*
1 *tablespoon canola oil*
1¹/₂ *cups chopped onions*
¹/₂ *teaspoon dried thyme*
2 *bay leaves*
2 *cups extra-long-grain white rice*
4 *cups chicken stock, preferably homemade*
Salt to taste
¹/₂ *teaspoon freshly ground black pepper*

1. Heat the butter and oil in a saucepan or sturdy casserole. When hot, add the onions, and sauté over medium to high heat for 2 to 3 minutes. Stir in the thyme, bay leaves, and rice, mixing until the rice is coated with the butter and oil.

2. Add the chicken stock, salt to taste, and the pepper. Bring to a strong boil, stirring occasionally, over high heat. Then reduce the heat to very low, cover with a tight-fitting lid, and cook for about 20 minutes, until the rice is tender and the liquid is absorbed.

3. Fluff the rice with a fork, and serve it immediately with the mussels.

YIELD: 6 SERVINGS

HOT CURRY WITH COOL FRUITS

Cheese and Tomato Salad
Sweet and Spicy Curried Chicken
Brown Rice and Onion Pilaf

ə

We love spicy food at our house, and the flavor of curry — occasionally with veal, sometimes with lamb, but most often with chicken — is always welcome.

My family prefers chicken legs to breasts, and that enables us to be generous with the white meat when we have guests. When I make a chicken stew for guests as well as family, however, I use just the legs, because the breast tends to dry out prepared this way. I buy either legs only or a whole chicken and bone it, reserving the breast to sauté skinless for another meal.

For the Sweet and Spicy Curried Chicken, I remove the skin from the chicken legs, thus eliminating many calories, some of them in the form of fat that would rise to the surface of the stew as it cooked. The skin of braised chicken also tends to shrivel and become unappetizingly rubbery.

To create a wonderful combination of sweet and hot flavors, I add apples and bananas along with sweet onions to intensify the contrast. The apples retain their shape better if they are not peeled, and the skin has a nice chewy texture.

continued

The Brown Rice and Onion Pilaf served with the chicken is one of my wife's favorites because she particularly likes the chewy texture of brown rice. Leftovers can be added to soup or sautéed as a thick pancake (see Special Tip, page 32).

I serve the Cheese and Tomato Salad throughout the year. In summer we take advantage of the fresh, ripe, round tomato varieties, but at other times we often use plum tomatoes instead; they are fleshy and don't have too many seeds.

I like beer better than wine with a spicy menu, but a Riesling or Gewürtztraminer would go well with this one, too.

CHEESE AND TOMATO SALAD

Make this salad ahead and let it macerate in the refrigerator until serving time. It will keep for several days. Leftovers can be added to soup or used as a terrific vegetarian sandwich filling or as a zesty addition to sandwiches containing meat.

1 1/2   pounds ripe tomatoes (regular or plum)

1 TO 2   onions (about 8 ounces total), peeled and cut into 1/2-inch cubes (about 1 1/2 cups)

1   cucumber (about 1/2 pound), peeled, cut in half lengthwise, seeded, and cut into 1/2-inch cubes (about 1 1/2 cups)

1/2   pound mozzarella cheese, cut into sticks about 1/2 inch thick by 1 1/2 inches long

1/2   cup shredded basil

1/4   cup chopped chives or parsley

1   teaspoon freshly ground black pepper

1   teaspoon salt

1/2   jalapeño pepper (optional), seeded and chopped fine (about 1 teaspoon)

3   tablespoons red wine vinegar

1/2   cup extra-virgin olive oil

1. Cut the tomatoes in half crosswise and gently squeeze out the seeds. Cut the seeded tomatoes into 1-inch pieces. Place the cut-up onions in a sieve and wash under cold water to remove some of the sulfurous compounds, which tend to make the onions discolor and are strong smelling and irritating to the eyes. Drain thoroughly.

2. Combine all the ingredients in a bowl, stirring well. Cover and refrigerate. Remove from the refrigerator an hour or so before serving, so the salad is cool, not cold, when eaten. Serve with a crunchy French bread.

YIELD: 6 SERVINGS

SWEET AND SPICY CURRIED CHICKEN

TOTAL TIME:

1 HOUR

Add more or less fruit to this dish, according to your own taste. Likewise with the curry mixture. Make your own curry powder or use a commercial brand—as is, if you prefer a mild flavor, or with added cumin and cayenne pepper if you like your seasonings piquant.

Mint lends a refreshing quality to the dish. Although fresh mint is usually available at the supermarket, you can substitute dried mint if necessary: Crumble it over the dish during the last few minutes of cooking.

1 *tablespoon unsalted butter*

1 *tablespoon canola oil*

6 *large chicken legs (about 4 pounds total), skin removed and legs split to separate the drumsticks from the thighs*

³/₄ *pound onions (3 to 4), peeled and diced (about 2¹/₂ cups)*

1 *tablespoon all-purpose flour*

2 *tablespoons curry powder*

1 *teaspoon cumin powder*

¹/₄ *teaspoon cayenne pepper*

1¹/₂ *teaspoons freshly ground black pepper*

1¹/₂ *teaspoons salt*

5 *cloves garlic, peeled, crushed, and coarsely chopped (about 1 tablespoon)*

1 *Granny Smith apple (about ¹/₂ pound), unpeeled, cut in half, seeded, and cut into 1-inch dice (about 1¹/₂ cups)*

1 *banana (about ¹/₂ pound), peeled and cut into ¹/₂-inch slices*

1 *large tomato, cut into 1-inch cubes (about 1 cup)*

2 *tablespoons shredded fresh mint or 1 teaspoon dried mint*

1. Heat the butter and oil in a large skillet. When hot, add the chicken and sauté (in a couple of batches, if necessary, to avoid crowding) over medium to high heat for a total of about 6 to 7 minutes, until brown on all sides. Transfer the chicken to a large casserole or Dutch oven and discard all but 2 to 3 tablespoons of the accumulated fat in the skillet.

2. Add the onions to the hot fat in the skillet and sauté for 2 to 3 minutes over medium heat, stirring. Then add the flour, curry powder, cumin powder, cayenne pepper, black pepper, salt, and garlic, and mix well with the onions. Add 1 cup water, stir, and bring to a boil. Pour the mixture over the chicken.

3. Add the apple, banana, and tomato, and bring to a boil over medium to high heat. Cover, reduce the heat, and simmer gently for about 25 to 30 minutes. Sprinkle the mint on top and serve immediately with the brown rice pilaf.

NOTE: The curried chicken is good reheated, but if you plan to make it ahead and reheat it at serving time, cook it only 20 minutes initially, instead of 30 minutes. By the time the dish is reheated, it will be cooked through.

YIELD: 6 SERVINGS

BROWN RICE AND ONION PILAF

I t is difficult to give an exact time or amount of liquid required to cook brown rice. While some brands cook in as little as twenty-five to thirty minutes, others require as long as one and a quarter hours and need substantially more liquid than is needed to cook white rice. When you have found a brand of brown rice that you particularly like, you can buy that brand exclusively and set up a recipe that works consistently.

TOTAL TIME:
ABOUT 1 HOUR

1 *tablespoon unsalted butter*

2 *tablespoons olive or vegetable oil*

³/₄ *pound onions (3 to 4), peeled and cut into ¹/₂-inch cubes (about 2¹/₂ cups)*

1 *teaspoon herbes de Provence (see Note, page 150) or Italian seasoning*

2 *cups brown rice (about 1 pound)*

2 *teaspoons salt*

¹/₂ *teaspoon freshly ground black pepper*

1. Heat the butter and oil in a large sturdy saucepan. When hot, add the onion and sauté over medium to high heat for about 2 to 3 minutes.

continued

Add the herbes de Provence and rice and mix well to combine. Add 5 cups water, the salt and pepper, and bring the mixture to a boil, stirring so it does not stick.

2. When the mixture is boiling, reduce the heat and cook, covered, over very low heat for about 40 minutes, until the rice is tender, but still a little chewy, and most of the moisture has been absorbed. Check the rice near the end of the cooking time; if it is not cooked through, cook it a little longer, adding additional water as needed. Serve with the curried chicken.

YIELD: 6 SERVINGS

*S*PECIAL TIP   RICE PANCAKES: *Make a rice pancake with leftover brown rice from the pilaf: Heat 2 tablespoons oil in a 7-inch nonstick skillet. When hot, add 1 1/2 cups of the cooked brown rice and press lightly with a spatula to flatten. Cook over medium heat for 5 to 6 minutes, then invert onto a flat pan lid and slide back into the skillet. Brown on the other side for 5 to 6 minutes.*

Serve plain or topped with a fried egg as a light luncheon entree, and accompany it with a green salad.

ONE CHICKEN, TWO DISHES

Chicken Diable
Cauliflower and Crumbs

☉

Lentil and Chicken Fricassee

☉

othing is as versatile and economical as chicken, especially when bought whole. If you compare the price of a whole bird and one that has been cut up, you'll find a dramatic difference. Merely splitting a chicken in half enables the purveyor to increase its cost at least 15 to 20 percent and, should you want to buy only the breasts and drumsticks, you'll find the price per pound has skyrocketed to more than double that of a whole chicken. Boned chicken pieces are, of course, costlier still.

From one whole chicken, I have created two very different dishes: a spicy, garlicky Chicken Diable with the meat, and a Lentil and Chicken Fricassee with the bones. Granted, a certain amount of common sense and a little work are required to cut up a chicken. Although I used a whole one for the two main-dish recipes here, you can substitute precut breasts and legs in the first recipe and packaged backs and gizzards in the second. Since this will raise the price of these dishes substantially, however, I encourage you to follow the instructions for boning a chicken.

continued

The Chicken Diable is a quick dish made by sautéeing the meat of the chicken and flavoring it with red wine vinegar, garlic, and tomato. The bones could be used to make brown as well as white stock (which can be frozen for later use in soups and sauces). Instead, they are browned here with the chicken gizzard, heart, and neck, then used as a base in which to cook lentils for the fricassee. Potatoes, white beans, or black-eyed peas could be substituted for the lentils.

Fulfilling and earthy, the fricassee can be served family style right from the pot. This way it is finger food: any remaining meat can be sucked from the bones at the table. It can also be presented more elegantly by removing the bones with a slotted spoon and setting them aside on a tray until they are cool enough to handle. Then the meat can be picked off the bones and added to the lentils.

The two chicken dishes should not be served as part of the same menu. Either the lentil dish can be made first and the chicken pieces kept in readiness for a coming dinner party, or the Chicken Diable can be prepared first and the bones frozen or made immediately into the fricassee, which can then be frozen.

A tasty complement to the Chicken Diable is steamed cauliflower coated with toasted bread crumbs and sautéed scallions and ginger. Because cauliflower can be costly, it's perfectly all right to use slightly wilted or older vegetables that are available at reduced prices. The dark spots on the floret tips can be cut away before the vegetable is steamed, and since the florets will be covered with the bread-crumb-and-scallion mixture, guests will be unaware of your trimming.

Another bonus here is the crackling, made from the skin of the chicken. Freshly baked crackling is very crunchy and makes a delicious garnish for the lentils. It can also be sprinkled on salads or substituted for bacon in a sandwich.

SPECIAL TIP: *The chicken liver is not used in either of these recipes — it is a treat for the cook to enjoy while preparing dinner. Split the liver in half, sprinkle it with a little salt and freshly ground pepper, and sauté it briefly (about 45 seconds) on each side in a dash of olive oil or butter. Place on a sliver of bread and enjoy with a sip of white wine.*

CHICKEN DIABLE

For an elegant family menu, serve the Chicken Diable and the cauli-flower with a simple salad and a vinegar-and-oil dressing. For a slightly less pungent sauce, substitute white wine for half the vinegar. Fruit makes a nice dessert, or, if you are having company, you might serve a fruit tart or ice cream.

TOTAL TIME: ABOUT 40 MINUTES PLUS 10 TO 30 MINUTES TO BONE CHICKEN, DEPENDING ON PROFICIENCY

1 *3¹/₂- to 4-pound chicken, including giblets*

2 *very ripe medium-size tomatoes (about 8 ounces)*

¹/₂ *teaspoon plus ¹/₈ teaspoon salt*

³/₄ *teaspoon coarsely ground black pepper*

1 *tablespoon olive oil*

1 *tablespoon unsalted butter*

4 *cloves garlic, peeled, crushed, and finely chopped (about 1 tablespoon)*

¹/₄ *cup red wine vinegar*

1 *tablespoon chopped tarragon or 2 tablespoons coarsely minced parsley, for garnish*

1. Bone the chicken by first cutting off the legs at the hip, where the skin is loose. Chop off the tips of the drumsticks, and reserve for the Lentil and Chicken Fricassee. Separate the drumsticks from the thighs. Cut off the wings, leaving the first joint attached to the breast. Reserve the wings for the fricassee. Then remove the wishbone by cutting along each side of it and pulling it out. Cut off the 2 breasts at the shoulder and along each side of the sternum, or breastbone. (The breasts should be boneless except for the little bones in the first joint of the wings.)

2. Pull off the skin and set it aside for crackling. Reserve with the bones and giblets for the chicken fricassee.

3. Peel the tomatoes with a knife after dipping them briefly into boiling water or holding them over the flame of a gas stove until the lightly browned skin slides off easily. Cut the tomatoes in half to expose the seeds and squeeze them out. Chop the tomato flesh. You should have about 1 cup. (The seeds, juice, and skin can be frozen for use in stock or added to the Lentil and Chicken Fricassee.)

continued

4. Sprinkle the 6 pieces of chicken with the $\frac{1}{2}$ teaspoon salt and $\frac{1}{2}$ teaspoon of the pepper.

5. Heat the oil and butter in a sturdy skillet (preferably of thick heavy copper or aluminum) with a lid. When hot, place the thighs and drumsticks in the pan, cover, and sauté over medium to high heat for 3 minutes. Turn the pieces over and cook, covered, for 3 more minutes. Add the breasts, cover again, and continue cooking for 5 minutes. Turn the breasts over, cover, and cook for 2 more minutes. Remove all the chicken pieces to a serving platter and keep warm.

6. Add the garlic to the drippings in the pan and stir for about 20 to 30 seconds, without browning. Add the vinegar, stirring with a flat wooden spatula to mix in all the solidified juices, and cook for about 1 to 2 minutes. All of the vinegar should have evaporated and only the juice and fat should remain.

7. Add $\frac{1}{4}$ cup water and the chopped tomatoes. Bring to a boil, then cover and boil over high heat for $1\frac{1}{2}$ minutes. Stir in the remaining $\frac{1}{8}$ teaspoon salt and $\frac{1}{4}$ teaspoon pepper.

8. Spoon the sauce over the chicken and garnish with the tarragon or parsley. Serve immediately.

NOTE: You can keep the chicken warm if it is ready a little ahead of time, but don't cover with the sauce and herbs until just before serving.

YIELD: 4 SERVINGS

CAULIFLOWER AND CRUMBS

Make your own bread crumbs in a food processor or blender using any stale or fresh bread. This is preferable to buying expensive packaged crumbs. Notice that the bread crumbs for this recipe are simply toasted, rather than sautéed, as they are traditionally, in highly caloric butter and oil.

TOTAL TIME: 30 MINUTES

1 *large cauliflower (about 1 1/2 pounds)*

About 1 cup fresh bread crumbs (see Special Tip, page 243)

1/4 *teaspoon salt*

1/4 *teaspoon freshly ground black pepper*

2 *tablespoons olive oil*

2 *tablespoons unsalted butter*

3 TO 4 *scallions, trimmed and minced (about 1/2 cup)*

2 *teaspoons finely chopped fresh ginger*

1. Clean the cauliflower: If there are discolored spots on top, cut them off, and separate the head into 14 to 16 flowerets. Peel off and discard the thick outside layer of the stem and split the stem into 2 or 3 pieces.

2. Place the flowerets in one layer in a large saucepan (preferably stainless steel) and add 1 1/2 cups water. Bring to a boil over high heat, cover, and boil for 6 to 8 minutes, until tender but still slightly firm. Drain the cauliflower, spread it out in one layer in the gratin dish in which it will be served, and set it aside until serving time.

3. Brown the crumbs by spreading them evenly on a small cookie sheet and placing it in a preheated toaster oven or under the preheated broiler in a conventional oven. Set aside.

4. At serving time, reheat the cauliflower in a microwave oven or place it in a saucepan with 4 to 5 tablespoons water, cover, bring to a boil, and boil for 2 to 3 minutes, until heated through. Arrange the cauliflower stems and flowerets, stem side down, in the gratin dish and sprinkle with the salt and pepper. Distribute the browned bread crumbs evenly over the top.

5. Heat the olive oil and butter in a skillet until hot. Add the scallions and ginger and cook for 20 to 30 seconds. Sprinkle on top of the crumb-covered cauliflower and serve immediately.

YIELD: 4 TO 6 SERVINGS

LENTIL AND CHICKEN FRICASSEE

TOTAL TIME:
1 HOUR AND
10 MINUTES TO
1 HOUR AND
40 MINUTES

Since the fricassee is made primarily from the bones of the chicken used in the Chicken Diable, it is a bonus dish, costing only the price of the lentils and vegetables. The dish can be frozen. Reheat it in the oven directly from the freezer, or defrost it overnight in the refrigerator and reheat gently on top of the stove, adding a little additional water.

The Lentil and Chicken Fricassee is excellent with a crunchy salad with garlic dressing and country-type bread. A good Beaujolais would be a welcome addition to this meal.

About 1 1/2 pounds chicken wings, bones, neck, fat, and
*   giblets leftover from Chicken Diable (page 35)*
2 carrots, peeled and cut into 1/2-inch pieces (about 1 cup)
1 large onion, peeled and cut into 1/2-inch pieces (about 1 cup)
3 cloves garlic, peeled, crushed, and coarsely chopped (about
*   1 teaspoon)*
1 teaspoon dried oregano
2 bay leaves
1 pound dried lentils, rinsed under cool water and drained
1 3/4 teaspoon salt
1/2 teaspoon freshly ground black pepper
Skin from 1 chicken (from Chicken Diable), in large pieces

1. Chop the chicken wings, bones, and neck into large pieces and place in a sturdy enamel or cast-iron pot along with the fat. Cut the gizzard and heart into 1/2-inch pieces and add to the pot. Cover and cook over medium to high heat for about 20 minutes, until the bones are nicely browned. (During the first 5 to 10 minutes of cooking, some liquid will come out of the bones and create steam, but eventually the bones will start to brown.)

2. Add the carrots, onion, garlic, oregano, and bay leaves, stir well, and cook for 1 minute.

3. Add the washed lentils to the bone mixture along with 8 cups water and 1 1/2 teaspoons of the salt. Bring the mixture to a strong boil, reduce the heat, and boil the mixture gently, covered, for about 45 minutes to 1 hour, or until the lentils are very tender and the liquid almost absorbed. Sprinkle with the pepper and stir to incorporate.

4. Meanwhile, make the crackling by spreading the pieces of chicken skin (outer surface up) on a jelly-roll pan or other pan with sides to contain the fat. Sprinkle with the remaining 1/4 teaspoon salt and bake in a preheated 400-degree oven for 20 minutes. The skin will become nicely browned and dry. (Do not stir or move the pieces of skin while they cook; they should hold firmly to the bottom of the pan as they cook to assure that they remain completely flat and do not shrivel. The fat rendered from the skin can be used to sauté vegetables, meat, or fish.)

5. Crumble the crackling on top of the fricassee and serve.

YIELD: 4 TO 6 SERVINGS

SENTIMENTAL FAVORITES

Vegetable and Oatmeal Soup
Sausage and Potato Ragout
Escarole Salad

When I was growing up in France at the end of World War II, food was scarce and even ordinary staples were limited. Nevertheless, my mother's ingenuity enabled her to create memorable meals for our family. I still prepare variations on them today. The recipes in this menu are illustrative of my mother's imaginative cuisine, born of necessity.

Vegetable soup was common fare at our house in spring as well as winter. Often the vegetables were served in chunks as they are here; at other times, the cooked mixture was pureed before serving. The selection changed according to what was available—sometimes parsnips, sometimes cabbage, sometimes the combination used in this recipe: onions, scallions, and carrots. Generally, the soup was thickened with potato, leftover bread, or some other starch or grain such as couscous, barley, farina, or oatmeal.

Meat and potato ragout was one of my mother's standards. She sometimes made it, as I have here, with pieces of sausage. At other times, she used pieces of cured pork (unsmoked bacon) or leftover ham, and it could also be made with leftover roast pork, veal, or beef. Instead of ready-made hot Italian sausage, homemade sausage can be substituted.

The vegetable soup, comforting ragout, and salad make an ideal cool spring menu, but one that would also be excellent in fall or winter. A Zinfandel goes well here, and fruit provides a fine finish to the meal.

*S*PECIAL TIP: *If you have leftover ragout and soup, remove any remaining bay leaves from the ragout and place both mixtures in the bowl of a food processer. Process until pureed and pour back into a pot with enough water to create the consistency of a soup. Reheat and serve this new soup with croutons.*

VEGETABLE AND
OATMEAL SOUP

The old-fashioned type of oatmeal is used as the thickener in this recipe because it holds its shape well in the soup. However, if you prefer, quick-cooking oatmeal can be added instead at the last moment. The soup is made with water, rather than stock, because water preserves the taste of fresh vegetables well. As children, my brothers and I added milk to the hot mixture in our bowls to cool it, a common practice when dining at home in France.

TOTAL TIME: ABOUT 45 MINUTES

2 *tablespoons safflower oil*

3 *small onions (about 8 ounces), peeled and cut into 1-inch dice (about 1 1/2 cups)*

4 *scallions, cleaned and cut into 1/2-inch pieces (about 1 1/4 cups)*

3 *medium-size carrots, peeled and cut into 1/2-inch dice (about 1 1/4 cups)*

1 *cup old-fashioned oatmeal*

1 *teaspoon salt*

1/4 *teaspoon freshly ground black pepper*

1. Heat the oil in a sturdy saucepan, preferably stainless steel. When hot, add the onions, scallions, and carrots, and cook, stirring, over high heat for about 3 minutes.

2. Add 7 cups water, and bring to a boil. Reduce the heat, cover, and boil gently for 10 minutes.

3. Add the oatmeal and salt, and bring to a boil again. Cover and cook for 5 minutes. Add the pepper and serve immediately, or set aside and reheat later.

YIELD: 6 SERVINGS

SAUSAGE AND POTATO RAGOUT

TOTAL TIME:
65 MINUTES

If you decide to make your own sausage, grind the meat from one and a half pounds of pork shoulder, season it to your liking with black pepper, cayenne pepper, salt, red wine, and anise, and form it into two dozen plum-sized balls.

In the drippings of the sausage, I make a light roux, which gives smoothness and body to the ragout. Both the potatoes and onions should be in large chunks so they don't cook down to a puree. At the end of the cooking time, remove the lid of the pot if necessary to let some of the liquid evaporate so just enough moisture remains to form a light, creamy sauce. The ragout is delicious served with a dollop of spicy mustard and a garlicky salad.

1½ *pounds ready-made hot Italian sausage (about 6 sausages) or homemade sausage (see above)*

1½ *tablespoons all-purpose flour*

3 *pounds potatoes, peeled and cut into 2-inch pieces*

4 *medium-size onions (about 1 pound), peeled and cut into 2-inch pieces*

5 *cloves garlic, peeled and thinly sliced (about ⅓ cup)*

3 *bay leaves*

1 *teaspoon dried thyme*

½ *jalapeño pepper, chopped, or more to taste (optional)*

¾ *teaspoon salt*

¼ *teaspoon freshly ground black pepper*

2 *tablespoons chopped parsley*

1. Cut each sausage into 4 or 5 pieces (there should be about 24 pieces in all). Place them in one layer in a large saucepan, add ½ cup water, bring to a boil, cover, and cook over medium heat for about 8 minutes. Uncover and cook over high heat for 1 to 2 minutes, until the water has evaporated and the sausages sizzle in their own fat.

2. Add the flour, stir well, and cook for about 1 minute, until the flour browns lightly in the fat. Add 2 cups water, stir well, and bring to a boil. Add the remainder of the ingredients except the parsley, and bring to a boil. Cover, reduce the heat to low, and continue cooking for about

30 minutes. When you serve the dish, there should be just enough liquid remaining in the pan to moisten the potatoes. If necessary, continue cooking, uncovered, over high heat for 2 to 3 minutes to reduce the liquid and create a creamy sauce.

3. Sprinkle with the parsley, and serve immediately.

NOTE: Add a little water to the ragout to reheat it in a microwave oven without sticking. To reheat it conventionally, put the ragout in a pan with a little water, and warm it, stirring occasionally, over low heat until it is heated through.

YIELD: 6 SERVINGS

ESCAROLE SALAD

TOTAL TIME:
12 TO 15
MINUTES

Use escarole that is firm and white inside, indicating tenderness and sweetness, even if the outer leaves are slightly damaged. The tougher outer leaves can be reserved and added with the scallions to the soup. You can double or triple the dressing recipe, and store what is left over, tightly covered, in the refrigerator, where it will keep for a week or so.

Remember to serve the salad in a bowl large enough to allow the greens to be tossed with the dressing at serving time without spilling over.

1 TO 2 *heads escarole (about 8 cups cleaned greens)*

FOR THE DRESSING

2 *cloves garlic, peeled, crushed, and chopped fine or put through a garlic press (about 1 teaspoon)*

¹/₂ *teaspoon salt*

¹/₂ *teaspoon freshly ground black pepper*

1 *tablespoon Dijon-style mustard, preferably hot*

1 *tablespoon red wine vinegar*

3 *tablespoons safflower, corn, or canola oil*

1. To prepare the escarole, pull off the damaged or dark green outer leaves. (Although a little tough and bitter, these can be added to the Vegetable and Oatmeal Soup.) Wash the tender inner leaves carefully in a sink full of cold water, lifting them in and out of the water, then dry thoroughly, preferably in a salad spinner. It is important to remove all the water from the greens because any remaining on the leaves will dilute the dressing. Refrigerate until serving time.

2. *For the dressing:* Place the garlic, salt, pepper, mustard, and wine vinegar in the bowl in which the salad will be served (or use a jar if you are making extra dressing). Mix well with a spoon, and stir in the oil.

3. At serving time, toss the greens with the dressing. Serve with the Sausage and Potato Ragout.

YIELD: 6 SERVINGS

SALUTE TO SPRING

Garlicky Romaine with Croutons
Red Beans and Pork
Yellow Rice with Achiote
Guava with Cream Cheese and Mint

This menu begins with a light, tangy, green salad that is intended to shake us free of winter and open the door to spring. In contrast, the next course is an earthy, filling beans and pork concoction drawn from my wife's Puerto Rican heritage and similar to a dish she prepares often at home. Two more dishes boast tropical origins: rice colored and flavored with achiote, and, to finish, a classic treat of guava paste, sliced and served with cream cheese on crackers. This last is an old favorite given a new twist here — a garnish of refreshing leaves of fresh mint.

The beans are cooked with an inexpensive cut of pork from the shoulder or with country-style ribs, which are the ribs at the end of the loin toward the shoulder. The pork is cut into pieces, bones and all, browned with onions, and flavored with tomatoes, bay leaves, garlic, and jalapeño peppers, which are always available at my house since my wife buys them fresh and freezes them whole. Whenever she needs hot peppers for a dish, she retrieves them from the freezer and chops them while still frozen.

continued

Another essential seasoning that give the beans and pork dish an authentic flavor is coriander. I usually reserve the coriander leaves (cilantro) to use as a garnish on top of the dish, but I finely chop all the stems and root ends and add them to the beans when they are cooking. They impart a very special taste to the dish.

The yellow rice contains achiote, which are annatto seeds — the same type of seeds that American Indians used to crush and use as a coloring to paint their faces red. They are available bottled in the spice section of most supermarkets and are often used in expensive restaurants as a substitute for saffron to color rather than flavor the rice, since achiote doesn't have much flavor on its own.

I would suggest beer rather than wine with this menu. Puerto Rican beer is a good choice if it's available. If not, any full-flavored beer — perhaps a Mexican variety — would go well with the meal.

GARLICKY ROMAINE
WITH CROUTONS

I make this salad starter with Romaine lettuce because it holds up well to the garlicky dressing with mustard. I also like to make my croutons with leftover French-style bread, which makes a chewy crouton that is in tune with this type of salad.

TOTAL TIME:
15 MINUTES

FOR THE CROUTONS

3 *tablespoons peanut or corn oil*

2¹/₂ *cups diced (³/₄-inch) leftover French bread*

3 TO 4 *cloves garlic, peeled, crushed, and chopped fine (about 1 tablespoon)*

¹/₂ *teaspoon salt*

¹/₂ *teaspoon freshly ground black pepper*

1 *tablespoon Dijon-style mustard*

2 *tablespoons red wine vinegar*

¹/₃ *cup peanut or corn oil*

1 *head Romaine lettuce (about 1¹/₄ pounds), damaged leaves removed, cut into 1¹/₂-inch pieces, washed thoroughly, and dried in a salad spinner (about 12 cups, lightly packed)*

1. *For the croutons:* heat the oil in a large skillet. When hot, add the diced bread and sauté for about 4 minutes, until nicely browned on all sides. Remove from the skillet and set aside.

2. Combine the garlic, salt, pepper, mustard, vinegar, and oil in a bowl suitable for serving the salad.

3. When ready to serve, add the lettuce to the bowl and toss it with the dressing. Sprinkle with the croutons and serve immediately.

YIELD: 6 SERVINGS

Red Beans and Pork

TOTAL TIME:
3½ HOURS

Traditionally, dried beans are pre-soaked before cooking, but I just wash them thoroughly and remove any damaged beans and foreign materials. Soaking is not necessary providing the beans are started cooking in cool water.

The advantage to this type of dish is that it can be made ahead, and it is even better reheated the following day. It will keep for several days refrigerated and it freezes very well. It is especially good when reheated with the yellow rice, and the leftovers can be transformed into a delicious soup (see Special Tip, page 51).

2 *tablespoons corn or safflower oil*

2¼ *pounds pork shoulder or country-style ribs, bones and all cut into 2-inch pieces*

1½ *pounds dried red kidney beans*

4 *medium-size onions (about 1½ pounds), peeled and cut into 1-inch pieces (about 4½ cups)*

3 TO 4 *large bay leaves*

1½ *tablespoons dried oregano*

6 TO 8 *cloves garlic, peeled, crushed, and chopped fine (about 2 tablespoons)*

1 TO 2 *jalapeño peppers, depending on your tolerance for hotness, chopped with or without the seeds (which intensify the heat) (about 1½ tablespoons)*

4 TO 5 *plum tomatoes (about 1 pound), cut into ½-inch pieces (about 3 cups)*

1 *tablespoon salt*

1 *bunch coriander (cilantro) ½ cup leaves reserved and the remainder, including stems and roots, chopped (about ¾ cup)*

1. Heat the oil in a large Dutch oven or heavy casserole. When hot, add the meat and brown it over medium to high heat for about 20 minutes, turning occasionally, until well browned on all sides.

2. Meanwhile, put the beans in a sieve and rinse under cold water. Set them aside.

3. Add the onions to the browned pork and cook them for 4 to 5 minutes. Remove the pan from the heat and stir in the bay leaves, oregano, garlic, peppers, and tomatoes. Mix well and add 9 cups cold water, the salt, the chopped coriander and the beans. Bring to a boil, cover tightly, reduce the heat, and boil gently for about $2^{1}/_{2}$ hours, until the beans and pork are very tender.

4. Sprinkle with the reserved coriander leaves and serve with the Yellow Rice with Achiote.

YIELD: 6 TO 8 SERVINGS

SPECIAL TIP   RED BEANS AND PORK SOUP: *Remove any bones from the leftover meat and puree the remainder of the rice and beans in a food processor, adding a little water to thin it and a dash of salt, if needed. Garnish this flavorful hot sout with cilantro.*

Yellow Rice with Achiote

TOTAL TIME:
30 MINUTES

Often annatto seeds are placed in hot oil, and within a minute or so, they release their color into the oil. The seeds can be discarded at this point and the rice sautéed in the colored oil, or the seeds can be left in and eaten along with the rice. Another way of using the seeds—the procedure I usually follow when making this dish—is to pulverize them in a mini-chop or pound them in a mortar with a pestle to a powder and blended with the rice.

3 *tablespoons peanut or safflower oil*

2 *teaspoons achiote (annatto seeds), pounded lightly in a mortar and pestle, pulverized in a mini-chop, or left whole (see above)*

2 *onions (about 10 ounces), peeled and coarsely chopped*

2 *teaspoons dried oregano*

2 *cups Carolina-style rice*

1½ *teaspoons salt*

Tabasco sauce (optional)

1. Heat the oil in a saucepan. Add the achiote and cook for about 1 minute. The oil will become very yellow. (At this point, if you are using whole annatto seeds, remove and discard them if you prefer.) Add the onions and oregano and cook for 2 minutes over medium heat.

2. Add the rice, mix well, and stir in the salt and 4 cups water. Bring the mixture to a boil over medium to high heat, stirring occasionally. As soon as it boils, cover tightly, reduce the heat to very low, and cook for 20 minutes.

3. Serve with the Red Beans and Pork, arranging the beans and pork on top of or alongside the rice. Pass some Tabasco sauce if you like your food very hot.

NOTE: When you grind achiote in a mini-chop or crush it in a mortar, it will color the receptacle. One way to remove this color is to rub the interior surface with a dampened sponge dipped in a cleaner containing a little bleach and then wash the container in warm, soapy water. Rinse the bowl or mortar thoroughly in cool water.

YIELD: 6 SERVINGS

GUAVA WITH
CREAM CHEESE AND MINT

TOTAL TIME:
10 MINUTES

Guava paste, available commercially at most supermarkets in cans or packages, is vastly superior in the canned version, as the packaged varieties are a pale yellow color and contain added egg whites. Once opened, a can of guava paste can be kept for several weeks in the refrigerator. Guava paste and cream cheese makes a great snack as well as a dessert.

1 *8-ounce package cream cheese, cut into thin slices (about ¹/4 ounce each)*

2 *dozen Ritz or club-type crackers*

1 *1¹/2-pound can guava paste, cut into thin slices (about ¹/2 ounce each)*

2 *dozen mint leaves, for garnish*

1. Place a small slice of cream cheese on each cracker. Top with a small slice of guava paste and garnish with a mint leaf. Arrange the crackers on a plate and refrigerate until serving time.

YIELD: 6 SERVINGS

SUNDAY SUPPER

Gratin of Eggs and Spinach
Lamb Navarin
Choux à la Crème

Spring, for me, always brings visions of pale, tender, baby or spring lamb, as well as eggs in both main dishes and desserts. This diversified, elegant menu makes a great Sunday family meal.

Because of widespread concern over cholesterol, egg dishes rarely appear in most people's diets nowadays. Yet eggs—one of the richest sources of protein—are highly nutritious, constituting almost a complete food in themselves.

I use a modest amount, one egg per person, in the Gratin of Eggs and Spinach, and even fewer in the dessert. The gratin is served as the first course in this simple but sophisticated menu, but it would also make a great main course for lunch or a light supper, and is ideal for brunch. It can be made and assembled ahead.

The navarin of lamb is made with lamb breast, including bones and cartilage. This cut is usually available inexpensively at the supermarket; if you don't see it displayed with the meats, ask the butcher if he has a lamb breast in the back. Juicy and flavorful when stewed, the breast is a better selection for the navarin than the leg, which would be much more costly and not nearly as moist prepared this way.

The dessert is a classic: cream puffs stuffed with whipped cream and served with chocolate sauce. This is a sophisticated home dessert, particularly good if it's served right after it's made.

With this menu, you might serve a good-quality, inexpensive Spanish wine; Marques de Caceres, for example, would go well with the hearty lamb stew.

GRATIN OF EGGS AND SPINACH

TOTAL TIME:
35 MINUTES

If you make the gratin ahead of time, reheat it in a 425-degree oven for about 7 or 8 minutes to ensure that it is hot throughout before sliding it under the broiler. If you're serving it immediately after assembling it, while the spinach and cream sauce are still warm, simply place it under the broiler for a few minutes.

Fresh spinach (still wet from washing) sautéed in oil makes an excellent vegetable on its own, seasoned only with a little salt and pepper.

6 *large eggs*

1½ *tablespoons olive oil*

1 *pound spinach, washed and drained (about 16 cups)*

¼ *teaspoon salt*

¼ *teaspoon freshly ground black pepper*

FOR THE SAUCE

1½ *tablespoons unsalted butter*

1½ *tablespoons all-purpose flour*

1½ *cups cold milk*

¼ *teaspoon salt*

¼ *teaspoon freshly ground black pepper*

1½ *tablespoons grated Parmesan cheese*

1. Place the eggs in a saucepan and cover with warm tap water. Bring to a boil over high heat, reduce the heat, and boil gently for approximately 8 minutes. Pour off the hot water, and shake the eggs in the pan to crack the shells. Add some ice to the pan, and fill it with cold water. Set aside until the eggs are cool enough to handle, and then shell them. Return the eggs to the cool water, and set aside to cool completely.

2. Heat the olive oil in a skillet. When hot, add the spinach, still wet from washing, and press it into the skillet. Add the salt and pepper, and cook until the spinach is soft and wilted, about 3 minutes. Spread the spinach evenly in a gratin dish. Slice the eggs with an egg slicer or by hand, and arrange them in one layer on top of the spinach.

3. *For the sauce:* Melt the butter in a small saucepan. Add the flour, and mix it in with a whisk. Add the milk and bring to a boil, stirring (especially in the corners, where the mixture tends to stick and burn) until it comes to a boil. Stir in the salt and pepper, and continue to boil for about 10 seconds. Pour the sauce over the eggs, and sprinkle them with the cheese.

4. Place the gratin dish under a hot broiler for about 5 minutes, until the surface is nicely browned.

YIELD: 6 SERVINGS

PECIAL TIP: *It is important when preparing hard-cooked eggs to boil the eggs very gently; if they are cooked in rapidly boiling water, the whites become tough and rubbery. Then, immediately after the eggs are cooked, pour out the hot water, replace it with ice-cold water, and let the eggs remain in that water until they are completely cold. This prevents the outer part of the yolk from turning green and eliminates the strong smell of sulphur that is often associated with hard-cooked eggs.*

LAMB NAVARIN

TOTAL TIME:

1½ HOURS

You can make the navarin ahead of time, up to the point of adding the peas, which should be stirred in when the dish is reheated at the last moment so they don't lose their bright green color.

2 *lamb breasts (about 3 pounds total)*
2 *tablespoons all-purpose flour*
1 *large onion, peeled and cut into 1-inch dice (about 1½ cups)*
8 *cloves garlic, peeled and sliced thin (about 3 tablespoons)*
1½ *teaspoons salt*
¾ *teaspoon freshly ground black pepper*
1 *teaspoon herbes de Provence or Italian seasoning*
1½ *pounds potatoes, peeled and cut into 2-inch chunks*
¾ *pound carrots, peeled and cut into 2-inch lengths*
1 *10-ounce package frozen baby peas*
2 *tablespoons chopped parsley*

1. Cut the lamb between the rib bones into strips about 1½ inches wide. You should have about 14 pieces.

2. Place the lamb, preferably in one layer, in a large saucepan or Dutch oven and cook, turning occasionally, over medium heat, partially covered, for 30 minutes, until it has released most of its fat and is nicely browned on all sides. Remove the lamb to a plate and pour out and discard the fat. (You may have up to 1 cup of fat).

3. Return the meat to the pot, sprinkle it with the flour, and mix well. Add the onions, garlic, 3 cups water, the salt, pepper, and herbes de Provence, mix well, and bring to a boil. Cover, reduce the heat to low, and cook for 30 minutes.

4. Add the potatoes and carrots, and cook, covered, for 20 minutes. Then stir in the peas, and cook, covered, for 5 minutes.

5. To serve, spoon the navarin onto six individual plates and sprinkle with the parsley.

YIELD: 6 SERVINGS

CHOUX À LA CRÈME

This recipe makes six large puffs, one per person. You can, of course, make smaller puffs, cooking them a proportionately shorter time, and serve several per person. Small puffs, called profiteroles, are often stuffed with ice cream and served with hot chocolate sauce.

TOTAL TIME:
1 HOUR AND
40 MINUTES

A common mistake is to overcook the choux puffs and let them dry in the oven for too long. The puffs should not be like dry bread; they should hold their shape but be soft and moist inside. Traditionally, once the freshly baked choux have cooled a little, the tops are cut off and the soft centers pulled out and discarded before the puffs are stuffed. I prefer to leave this soft but cooked dough in place. Filled with blackberry preserves and whipped cream, the cream puffs are served on top of a very simple but particularly flavorful chocolate sauce made of melted chocolate and milk.

FOR THE CHOUX

3/4 cup water

1 tablespoon unsalted butter

1/8 teaspoon salt

3/4 cup all-purpose flour (approximately 3 3/4 ounces)

3 large eggs

FOR THE FILLING

1 1/2 cups heavy cream

1/4 cup confectioner's sugar

2 teaspoons pure vanilla extract

1/4 cup blackberry preserves

1 teaspoon confectioner's sugar, to dust the tops of the choux puffs

FOR THE CHOCOLATE SAUCE

8 ounces bittersweet or semisweet chocolate

1 1/4 cups milk

1. *For the choux:* Place the water, butter, and salt in a saucepan, and bring the mixture to a boil over high heat. Immediately remove from the heat, and add the flour all at once. Mix in the flour with a sturdy wooden spatula, return the pan to the stove over medium to high heat, and

stir until the mixture comes away from the sides of the pan and collects into one soft lump about the consistency of modeling clay. Cook for about 20 to 30 seconds, still stirring, to dry the mixture further. Remove from the heat and transfer to the bowl of a food processor. Process for 4 to 5 seconds to cool the mixture slightly.

2. Beat the eggs in a bowl with a fork until well mixed. Reserve 1 tablespoon of the beaten eggs to brush on the choux later, and add a third of the remaining egg mixture to the food processor bowl. Process for 5 to 6 seconds, just long enough to incorporate the eggs into the paste. Repeat with the remainder of the eggs, adding and incorporating half of them at a time. After the final addition, process the mixture for about 10 seconds, until very smooth.

3. Lightly butter a cookie sheet. Spoon 6 rounds of the dough, each about the size of a golf ball (approximately 3 tablespoons), onto the sheet, spacing them evenly to allow for expansion. Brush with the reserved tablespoon of beaten egg to smooth the tops and coat the surface of the balls.

4. Place the cookie sheet in a preheated 350-degree oven and bake for about 40 minutes, until the choux are nicely developed, lightly browned, and cooked through. The choux should hold their shape, but be soft, not like dry bread. Set aside in a draftfree spot on top of the stove.

5. *For the filling:* Place the cream, confectioner's sugar, and vanilla in a bowl, and whip until firm. Refrigerate until needed.

6. The dessert can be completed a few hours before serving. Remove and reserve the top of each choux puff, cutting around each puff about a quarter of the way down and lifting off the resulting cap. Either remove and discard some of the soft insides, or press this soft membrane against the walls of the choux. Spoon 2 teaspoons of the blackberry preserves into the base of each puff.

7. Spoon the reserved cream mixture into a pastry bag fitted with a star tip, and pipe it into the choux. Replace the caps, and sprinkle with the 1 teaspoon confectioner's sugar.

8. *For the chocolate sauce:* Heat the chocolate and milk in a saucepan over low to medium heat just until the chocolate melts. Mix well with a whisk, transfer to a bowl, and cool in the refrigerator, stirring occasionally.

9. Place a puff on each of six individual dessert plates. Serve with the chocolate sauce.

YIELD: 6 SERVINGS

A TRENCHERMAN'S DELIGHT

Stuffed Roast Veal Breast with Potatoes
Napa Cabbage Salad
Banana Ice Cream with Rum

Nothing braises and cooks better or produces better-flavored juices than veal. Although most veal is costly—especially scaloppine and roasts—veal breast is still relatively inexpensive. Stuffed and served in slices along with the soft, white cartilage bones, it makes a delicious, homey, festive dish that is great to enjoy with friends for a leisurely weekend dinner.

As children, my brother and I used to fight over the thin, translucent cartilage bones, with the winner getting to chew them up and swallow them! I still enjoy crunching on these bones at family gatherings, but some guests may be skittish at the prospect, so I suggest savoring this delicacy in the privacy of your own home with intimate trencherman friends.

Along with this vigorous, one-pot main dish is a refreshing salad composed of raw Napa cabbage, also known as celery cabbage or Chinese lettuce, tossed in a zesty dressing flavored with red wine vinegar, soy sauce, and garlic.

For dessert, a simple, lusty banana ice cream is perfect. Cut-up bananas are frozen and then combined with sour cream, sugar, and a little dark rum in a food processor to create a dense, rich ice cream. After hardening a little in the freezer, the ice cream is served as is or with a little more rum.

A French red table wine from Languedoc, in the south of France, would be a reasonably priced, appealingly fruity accompaniment to this menu.

STUFFED ROAST VEAL BREAST WITH POTATOES

TOTAL TIME:
2½ HOURS

The breast is stuffed with a sausage mixture that can be made with either sweet or hot sausage meat. I use the sweet mixture here, combining it with thick-crusted leftover bread, and flavoring it with onion, parsley, and garlic. The top of the gently roasted breast browns beautifully, and the potatoes take on the delicious flavor of the meat juices as they cook.

FOR THE STUFFING

2½ *cups stale coarse bread crumbs, preferably from a crusty country loaf*
1 *pound sweet Italian sausage meat*
¼ *cup chopped parsley*
½ *cup chopped onion*
1 *teaspoon freshly ground black pepper*
2 TO 3 *cloves garlic, peeled, crushed, and chopped (about 2 teaspoons)*

1 *3½- to 4-pound veal breast (4 to 5 ribs)*
1 *tablespoon olive oil*
1 *teaspoon salt*
1 *large onion (about 8 ounces), peeled and sliced*
2 *pounds medium-size potatoes (about 6), peeled and halved lengthwise*

1. *For the stuffing:* Mix all the ingredients together in a bowl.

2. Place the veal breast, meat side up, on a flat surface. Using a sharp, thin knife, cut a slit along the widest side of the breast, sliding your knife as close to the bones as possible, to create a deep pocket. Push the stuffing into the cavity and press on it to distribute it evenly over the bones. Tie the open end of the veal breast shut with soft kitchen string, wrapping it twice to secure the stuffing inside.

3. Heat the olive oil in a large casserole. Sprinkle the meat all over with the salt. When the oil is hot, brown the meat over medium heat for 30 minutes, turning occasionally so it is uniformly brown. Add the sliced onion and ½ cup water, cover, reduce the heat to very low, and cook for 1 hour.

4. Remove the meat to a platter. Arrange the potatoes in one layer in the juices (about 1½ cups) remaining in the casserole. Position the roast on top, meat side up, and cook, uncovered, in a preheated 400-degree oven for about 30 to 40 minutes, until the meat is nicely browned on top and the potatoes are cooked through.

5. At this point, the roast will be cooked enough so that the ribs can be twisted and pulled away from the meat. Slice the meat, following the shape of the ribs and slicing right through the cartilage bones. Serve 1 slice per person, with the potatoes and pan juices.

YIELD: 6 SERVINGS

𝒮 PECIAL TIP   SAUSAGE MEAT LOAF: *To make a delicious meat loaf, double the recipe for the stuffing, pack it into a loaf pan, and cook it, covered with aluminum foil, for 1¼ hours in a 350-degree oven. Garnish, if desired, with tomato sauce, and serve with mashed potatoes.*

Too fat with Bennie's sausage

Napa Cabbage Salad

TOTAL TIME:

12 MINUTES
Napa caggage resembles a pale, compact head of romaine lettuce. Delicately flavored, it makes a deliciously crunchy and unusual cole slaw. Wash the cabbage and prepare the dressing hours ahead if you like, and then mix them together 10 to 15 minutes before serving so the dressing softens the cabbage a little.

For the Dressing

2 TO 3 *cloves garlic, peeled, crushed, and chopped (about 2 teaspoons)*

$1/2$ *teaspoon salt*

$1/2$ *teaspoon freshly ground black pepper*

2 *teaspoons Dijon-style mustard*

1 *tablespoon red wine vinegar*

1 *tablespoon soy sauce*

3 *tablespoons canola oil*

1 *firm head Napa cabbage (about 1 pound)*

1. *For the dressing:* Place the garlic in a large salad bowl and mix in the remainder of the dressing ingredients.

2. Trim the cabbage, removing and discarding any damaged or wilted leaves, and cut the head crosswise into 1-inch slices. You should have about 8 cups. Wash well and spin dry in a salad spinner (any moisture would dilute the dressing).

3. About 10 to 15 minutes before serving, add the cabbage to the dressing, toss well, and set aside, so the dressing can penetrate the cabbage and soften it slightly.

YIELD: 6 SERVINGS

BANANA ICE CREAM WITH RUM

I prefer to use bananas when little black dots begin appearing on their skin, indicating they are ripe and at their flavor peak. Although this dessert can be made with bananas that are a little riper still (with larger black spots on the skin), don't wait too long; as the skin turns black, the fruit becomes mushy and somewhat grainy in texture.

TOTAL TIME:
15 MINUTES
PLUS 3 HOURS
FOR FREEZING

If the frozen banana pieces are very hard, let them soften briefly at room temperature so they can be pureed smoothly with the other ingredients.

For dessert lovers who are counting calories, yogurt can be substituted for the sour cream with good results.

5 *medium-size ripe bananas (about 2 pounds)*

3/4 *cup sour cream*

1/3 *cup sugar*

2 *tablespoons dark rum, plus 2 tablespoons (optional) to sprinkle on top at serving time*

6 *sprigs mint for garnish (optional)*

1. Peel the bananas and cut them crosswise into 1-inch slices. Arrange the slices in a single layer on a tray and place the tray in the freezer for at least 2 hours, or until the bananas are frozen.

2. Put half the frozen bananas in the bowl of a food processor with half the sour cream, half the sugar, and 1 tablespoon of the rum. Pulse the machine a few times, and then process the mixture for approximately 20 seconds, until smooth. Transfer to a cold bowl. Process the remaining bananas, sour cream, and sugar, with a second tablespoon of the rum, and add to the bowl. Place the ice cream in the freezer for at least 1 hour, or until serving time.

3. To serve, scoop the ice cream into six chilled glasses, and garnish each with 1 teaspoon rum and/or a sprig of mint, if desired.

YIELD: 6 SERVINGS

Summer

SUMMER SALAD BUFFET

Bean and Bacon Salad
Beet Salad
Pickled Vegetables Gerry

A PARTY PROVENÇAL

Grand Aïoli
Quick Fragrant Ratatouille
Strawberries with Sour Cream and Brown Sugar

THREE VEGETARIAN MENUS WITH PASTA

MENU 1.

Warm Vegetable Salad
Macaroni Beaucaire
Strawberry Summer Pudding

MENU 2.

Spaghetti with Basil Pesto
Herb-Stuffed Zucchini Boats
Honeyed Melon

MENU 3.

Zucchini-Yogurt Soup
Pasta Shells with Ricotta Filling
Strawberry and Orange Coupe

SUMMER PICKINGS

MENU 1.

Tomatoes on Garlic Toasts
Cod with Olives
Peaches in Red Wine

MENU 2.

Baked Chicken with Herb Crumbs
Tomatoes Provençal
Rhubarb Compote with Sour Cream

Tomatoes with Chicken Stuffing

TWO SUPPERS FROM THE GRILL

MENU 1.

Hot or Cold Leek Soup
Haddock on Polenta
Grilled Turkey Wings

MENU 2.

Flan of Green Herbs
Spicy Grilled Beef Roast
Swiss Chard Gratin

RUSSIAN CLASSIC, UPDATED

Tomato Salad with Red Onion and Basil
Salmon and Green Beans Pojarski
Parsley Potatoes

SUMMER SALAD BUFFET

Bean and Bacon Salad
Beet Salad
Pickled Vegetables Gerry

Summer dining is usually a casual affair for us, a time when we eat a lot of fish, more vegetables than meat, and, especially, a lot of salads. Often, when guests come for dinner, I prepare a buffet consisting of different types of salads, all of which can be eaten at room temperature.

The two salads and the pickled vegetables that make up this menu are ideal summer buffet fare. Fill out the menu with storebought foods: cheese, crunchy French bread, olives, nuts, and, if meat is desired, cold chicken or ham. I often buy a ready-to-eat picnic shoulder, sometimes poaching it again in 180-degree water to cover for about 1 hour, to make it even more tender before slicing and serving it. For dessert, I suggest a big basket of fresh fruit. Varied, colorful, and satisfying, this menu is easy on the cook when temperatures soar.

The Bean and Bacon Salad, served at room temperature here as part of a buffet, can also be eaten hot as a vegetable accompaniment to roast meat. The very flavorful Beet Salad makes good use of fresh beets, which are plentiful and very sweet at the height of summer.

continued

The pickled vegetables in this menu are marinated in a mixture of vinegar, water, salt, pickling spices, hot pepper, and fresh herbs — a combination that can be varied to suit personal taste or seasonal availability without losing the essentially wonderful flavor of the recipe.

With this type of meal, try a red Beaujolais served cool; chilling enhances its flavor and helps compensate for its lack of tannic acid. This light, fruity red wine goes well with summer meals.

BEAN AND BACON SALAD

TOTAL TIME:
2 HOURS
This recipe calls for small, white navy beans, but you can substitute any other variety, from kidney to Great Northern to pea.

If possible, buy a slab of bacon so it can be cut into the thick slices needed to make those little sticks called *lardons*. However, regular sliced bacon can be used, as well as ham rind, which I save and freeze whenever I trim a Virginia ham.

1 *pound dried navy beans*

1½ *teaspoons salt*

8 *ounces slab bacon, cut into ½-inch-thick lengths and then across into ½-inch lardons*

1 *medium-size onion (about 4 ounces), peeled and chopped (about 1 cup)*

6 *cloves garlic, peeled, crushed, and chopped (about 1 tablespoon)*

½ *cup chopped parsley*

3 *tablespoons red wine vinegar*

3 *tablespoons virgin olive oil*

1 *teaspoon freshly ground black pepper*

1. Wash the beans and remove and discard any damaged ones or any foreign material. Place the beans in a pot with 6 cups cold water and 1 teaspoon of the salt. Bring to a boil, cover, reduce the heat to low, and cook until tender, 1 to 1 1/2 hours. (There should be only a little water remaining in the pot.) Let cool to lukewarm. (See Note.)

2. Place the lardons in a saucepan and sauté over low heat, covered, for about 8 minutes. Add the onion and garlic and cook, stirring, for about 5 seconds. Add the contents of the saucepan, fat and all, to the beans (with their remaining cooking liquid). Add the remaining 1/2 teaspoon salt and the remainder of the ingredients and mix well. Serve at room temperature.

NOTE: I don't believe it is necessary to soak dried beans ahead; in fact, if beans are soaked overnight in water, as many recipes suggest, bubbles often form on the surface of the water, indicating that the beans are fermenting— making them a less than desirable component of any bean recipe. It is preferable to wash the beans, cover them with water containing a dash of salt, and cook them immediately.

YIELD: 6 GENEROUS SERVINGS

PECIAL TIP: *If you want to reduce the amount of fat in the Bean and Bacon Salad, use ham instead of bacon. Buy a couple of 1/2-inch-thick slices of ham, cut them into lardons, and sauté them in 1 tablespoon olive oil in a skillet for just 1 to 2 minutes (as part of Step 2) before proceeding.*

Beet Salad

TOTAL TIME:
ABOUT 1½
HOURS

Not quite as low in calories as most other vegetables (approximately 220 calories per pound), beets contain a lot of carbohydrates and protein. To help preserve their nutrients, it is best not to peel them or remove their roots before cooking.

If you have a microwave oven, by all means cook your beets in it, following the oven manufacturer's guidelines for proper procedure and cooking time. Otherwise, cook the beets in the conventional manner—on top of the stove—as I do here, perhaps doubling the recipe to conserve on energy since beets require long cooking. Be sure to protect your work surface with newspaper when peeling them and to wash your hands directly afterwards, since they stain whatever they touch. Seasoned with sour cream, red wine vinegar, a dash of sugar, and lots of sliced onion, they make a delightful vegetable salad.

3 TO 4 *large beets (about 1 ¾ pounds), leafy tops removed*

1 *medium-size onion (about 4 ounces), peeled, halved, and very thinly sliced*

½ *cup sour cream*

3 *tablespoons red wine vinegar*

½ *teaspoon freshly ground black pepper*

2 *teaspoons sugar*

1 *teaspoon salt*

1. Place the beets in a large saucepan, cover with tepid tap water, and bring to a boil over high heat. Reduce the heat to low, cover with a lid, and cook gently for approximately 1 ¼ to 1 ½ hours, until tender. Drain and cool to lukewarm.

2. Peel the beets and cut them into ¼-inch slices. Place in a bowl and stir in the remaining ingredients. Serve at room temperature, but not cold.

YIELD: 6 SERVINGS

PICKLED VEGETABLES GERRY

If you like, tarragon and other fresh herbs can replace the dill and oregano in the marinade. If you don't have the commercial pickling spice mixture on hand, substitute dried thyme, black peppercorns, pieces of bay leaves, and coriander seeds. And although I include carrots, zucchini, broccoli, cauliflower, and onion, you can use other fresh vegetables you have on hand. These pickled vegetables always add interest to a buffet table and make a good accompaniment for meat, sandwiches, or such. They are ready to eat after five to six days in the marinade and will keep for weeks in the refrigerator.

TOTAL TIME: 12 MINUTES

1   *cup distilled white vinegar*
1¼ *cups water*
1½ *tablespoons salt*
1   *teaspoon pickling spices*
2   *dried hot peppers*
2   *sprigs dill or oregano*
3   *cloves garlic, peeled*

VEGETABLES (ENOUGH IN COMBINATION TO FILL A 1-QUART JAR)
4 OR 5   *green tomatoes, halved*
A few small carrots, cut into 2-inch sticks
A few small zucchini, cut into 2-inch chunks
Several broccoli or cauliflower flowerets
A few wedges of onion

1. Place the vinegar, water, salt, pickling spices, hot peppers, dill, and garlic in a saucepan and bring to a boil. Meanwhile, layer the vegetables in a 1-quart jar.

2. Pour the boiling liquid over the vegetables. Seal the jar, cool, and refrigerate for 5 to 6 days before serving. This mixture will keep, refrigerated, for several weeks.

YIELD: 6 SERVINGS

A PARTY PROVENÇAL

Grand Aïoli
Quick Fragrant Ratatouille
Strawberries with Sour Cream and Brown Sugar

❧

I can't think of another dish that lends itself better to an informal party than a grand aïoli. It is easy to make and colorful, and there are countless variations with vegetables, fish, and meat. Aïoli, the mayonnaise mixture at the center, is not for the timid nibbler; with its high concentration of garlic (at least one clove per person), it is a very assertive dish. So it is best eaten among friends and accompanied by generous glasses of dry, cool Provençal rosé. To aid digestion afterward, a game of *pétanque*, the famous French bowling game, does wonders.

According to Alphonse Daudet, a nineteenth-century author from Provence, aïoli will protect you from any sickness, and even from death. Legends surround the stirring of the aïoli (done in a food processor in my version, but conventionally mixed with a mortar and pestle): It was said that stirring the aïoli the wrong way (counterclockwise) would cause it to curdle. Among the other historical explanations for failed aïoli were that the garlic had germinated—or that the aïoli maker had an unfaithful spouse.

continued

This dish is made in two parts: garlic-laden aïoli that is the flavoring and spirit of the dish, and what I call the Grand Aïoli, the garnishes that form the base of the recipe. These include poached salted codfish, poached squid, an assortment of vegetables (including broccoli, zucchini, carrots, and potatoes), and hard-cooked eggs. Salted codfish, the main ingredient, is available in supermarkets. It usually comes from Nova Scotia, Canada, or Portugal, packed in wooden boxes or vacuum-packed in plastic.

Land snails are a common ingredient in the traditional versions of grand aïoli served in Marseilles and Provence. Since these are rarely available in this country, however, they aren't included in this version. Some recipes advise using small octopi in addition to the squid, while others suggest chicken and beef, and still others expand the vegetable suggestions to beets, cauliflower, string beans, artichokes, chick peas, and celery.

Although almost a meal in itself, the Grand Aïoli is followed here by another famous dish from Provence, ratatouille. This stew of onions, zucchini, green pepper, eggplant, tomatoes, and garlic sautéed in olive oil is superb in summer. Garnished with olive oil, black olives, and a sprinkling of black pepper, ratatouille is often served cold as an hors d'oeuvre. Taste carefully, however, if you are serving it cold—it may require additional salt. It will keep for several days in the refrigerator.

The simple dessert of strawberries served with sour cream and brown sugar is excellent, especially when the strawberries are very ripe.

With this Provençal menu, try a white wine or a chilled dry rosé, like Tavel, from the same region, along with a crusty French bread.

GRAND AÏOLI

Because of widespread concern over the possibility of salmonella contamination from raw eggs, I have eliminated egg yolks, the conventional binder, from the aïoli, replacing them with a little commercial mayonnaise. It is important that you use good-quality olive oil, either virgin or extra virgin, and that it be at room temperature; cold oil would cause the mixture to separate.

I wash the salted codfish well under cool water, and then blanch it before I cook it in a lot of unsalted boiling water. Taste the fish after blanching it, though; if it is still salty, blanch it a second time.

TOTAL TIME:
2 HOURS
(INCLUDING
½ HOUR TO CLEAN
THE SQUID)

FOR THE AÏOLI

1½ *slices white bread*

6 TO 8 *cloves garlic, peeled*

¼ *cup milk*

½ *cup commercial mayonnaise*

1 *tablespoon red wine vinegar*

½ *teaspoon freshly ground black pepper*

⅛ *teaspoon cayenne pepper*

½ *teaspoon salt*

1¼ *cups extra-virgin olive oil, at room temperature*

FOR THE GRAND AÏOLI

2 *pounds salted codfish*

2 *pounds small squid (about 18 to 20; this will yield about 1 pound 10 ounces cleaned)*

12 *small potatoes (about 1¾ pounds), thoroughly cleaned under cold water*

½ *teaspoon salt*

8 *carrots (about 1¼ pounds), trimmed and peeled*

1¾ *pounds broccoli, cut into flowerets, the stems peeled and the flowerets cut in half lengthwise*

3 *zucchini (about 1½ pounds), washed, trimmed at both ends, and cut into quarters lengthwise*

6 *hard-cooked eggs, shelled*

continued

1. *For the aïoli:* Place the bread and garlic in the bowl of a food processor and process for 10 to 15 seconds, until the garlic is thoroughly chopped. Add the milk, mayonnaise, vinegar, black pepper, cayenne, and salt, and process for a few seconds. With the processor running, pour the oil in a steady stream through the feed tube and process until the mixture is homogenized and thick. Cover and set aside at room temperature until serving time.

2. *For the grand aïoli:* Rinse the codfish thoroughly under cold water. Then place in a large saucepan and cover with 3 quarts cold water. Bring to a strong boil, boil for 30 seconds, and drain carefully. Rinse the fish thoroughly under cold water again, and remove any visible sinew or bones. Divide the fish into 6 pieces, place in a bowl of cold water, and set aside.

3. Remove the heads and tentacles from the squid, cutting the tentacles off just below the eyes and removing the beak inside. Press on the body to remove the soft mass inside. Remove the pen, the long plasticlike backbone inside the body, and as much of the black exterior skin as you can. Rinse thoroughly under cold water and set aside.

4. Place the potatoes in a saucepan, cover with cold water, and bring to a boil. Cover, reduce the heat, and cook until tender when pierced with a fork, about 20 minutes. Drain and set aside in the pan to dry.

5. At serving time, bring 2 cups water to a boil in a saucepan. Add the salt and the cleaned squid. Bring to a boil, reduce the heat, and simmer for about 3 minutes. Drain and set aside.

6. Bring 2 quarts of water to a boil in a saucepan, add the codfish, return the water to a boil, and simmer for 2 minutes. Remove from the heat and let the codfish stand in the water for 5 to 10 minutes; drain the codfish just before serving.

7. Meanwhile, place the carrots in a saucepan with cold water to cover, and bring to a boil. Boil for 8 to 12 minutes or until tender, and then lift the carrots from the water with a slotted spoon and set aside. Add the broccoli to the water and return it to the boil. Cook for 3 minutes, then remove the broccoli with a skimmer and set aside. Drop the zucchini into the water, return the water to the boil, and cook the zucchini for 30 seconds. Remove it with a skimmer and set aside.

8. Reheat the peeled hard-cooked eggs and the cooked potatoes by placing them momentarily in the hot water with the salted codfish.

9. To serve, arrange the codfish on a platter and surround it with the squid, vegetables, and hard-cooked eggs. Serve immediately with the aïoli and crunchy French bread.

NOTE: Most of the vegetables for the Grand Aïoli can be cooked ahead and reheated in a microwave oven or on top of the stove. Add a few tablespoons of water to the vegetables for the stovetop method to provide some additional moisture. The broccoli and zucchini can be cooked at the last minute with the squid while you are finishing the codfish.

The eggs can be hard-cooked ahead, too, but should be placed under ice-cold water immediately after cooking to prevent the outer part of the yolks from developing a greenish tint.

YIELD: 6 SERVINGS

QUICK FRAGRANT RATATOUILLE

TOTAL TIME:
ABOUT 1 HOUR

The cooking time for this ratatouille is less than that for more traditional versions of this dish, with the tomatoes and garlic added only in the
last few minutes; this method helps retain the color, texture, and individual
flavors of the vegetables.

¼ *cup virgin or extra-virgin olive oil, plus extra for garnish*

3 *onions (about 1 pound), peeled and cut into 1-inch pieces
(about 3 cups)*

1 *large green bell pepper (about ½ pound), cut in half, cored,
seeded, and cut into ½-inch pieces (about 1½ cups)*

1 *large eggplant (about 1 pound), trimmed at both ends and
cut into 1-inch pieces (about 6 cups)*

4 *small zucchini (about 1¼ pounds), trimmed at both ends
and cut into 1-inch pieces (about 4 cups)*

¼ *teaspoon red pepper flakes*

1½ *teaspoons salt*

6 TO 8 *cloves garlic, peeled and sliced (about 3 tablespoons)*

4 *tomatoes (about 1½ pounds), cut into 1-inch cubes (about
4 cups)*

1 *cup shredded basil*

Freshly ground black pepper, for garnish

1. Heat the oil in a large saucepan. When hot, add the onions and
green pepper, and sauté for about 5 minutes over high heat. Then add the
eggplant, zucchini, red pepper flakes, and salt, reduce the heat to medium,
cover, and cook for 25 minutes, stirring occasionally to prevent the mixture
from sticking. (There is enough moisture in the vegetables to keep the mixture from burning.) Add the garlic and tomatoes and continue cooking,
covered, for 6 to 8 minutes.

2. Remove from the heat, transfer to a serving bowl, and cool to
room temperature.

3. Just before serving, stir half the basil into the ratatouille. Sprinkle
the remaining basil on top, and garnish with a few tablespoonfuls of olive
oil and a few grindings of black pepper.

NOTE: The ratatouille can also be served cold, garnished with additional basil.

YIELD: 6 SERVINGS

*S*PECIAL TIP: *Leftover ratatouille can be chopped fine into a "caviar," seasoned with a dash of hot pepper flakes or cayenne pepper, and served as a dip with potato chips, corn chips, or crackers. This mixture makes a great stuffing, too, for ravioli, which can be served with tomato sauce for a light lunch.*

STRAWBERRIES WITH SOUR CREAM AND BROWN SUGAR

Be sure to rinse the berries before they are hulled so water does not get inside them at the exposed stem end. Drain in a colander, hull, and refrigerate until serving time. If you prefer, serve the berries with sour cream only, eliminating the sprinkling of brown sugar.

TOTAL TIME: 10 MINUTES

1 *quart (1 3/4 pounds) ripe strawberries, washed and hulled*
1 *16-ounce container sour cream*
3/4 *cup light brown sugar*

1. Divide the strawberries among six individual dessert bowls. Spoon 2 to 3 generous tablespoons of the sour cream over the berries in each bowl and sprinkle each serving with 2 tablespoons of the brown sugar. Serve.

YIELD: 6 SERVINGS

THREE VEGETARIAN MENUS WITH PASTA

MENU 1.

Warm Vegetable Salad
Macaroni Beaucaire
Strawberry Summer Pudding

A completely vegetarian dinner, finished off with seasonal berries, is a refreshing change after the heavier diet of the cold winter months, and usually comes in response to thoughts of a slimmer self at the beach.

The Warm Vegetable Salad that starts this menu features zucchini, carrots, celery, cauliflower, and radishes, but feel free to substitute other vegetables that may be more readily available at your market.

I like to cook all the vegetables in the same unsalted water so I have the least possible loss of vitamins and nutrients. The stock that results from the cooking is terrific to drink, or it can be set aside in the refrigerator or freezer for later use in a soup or stew.

The gratin of macaroni is named after the small town in the south of France where I first tasted the dish that inspired this recipe. Even though it is served here as a main course, it could be used as a first course or as an accompaniment to a meat dish, anything from veal to rabbit to lamb.

When strawberries are in season, I like to use them in a Strawberry Summer Pudding, a type of dessert the British are so good at making. My version is simply a mixture of strawberries liquified in a food processor and sweetened with strawberry jam and sugar, then combined with just enough bread crumbs so that the mixture holds together in a pudding. I serve it on additional sliced berries that have been sweetened with sugar.

With this vegetarian menu, I suggest a cold, dry rosé wine such as Côtes de Provence, from the south of France.

Warm Vegetable Salad

TOTAL TIME:
20 MINUTES

This salad is particularly good served at room temperature or slightly warm. If prepared ahead, warm it for a few seconds in a microwave oven or conventional oven to take the chill off before serving.

4 *small zucchini (about 1 pound)*

4 *medium carrots (about 10 ounces)*

4 *stalks celery (about 6 ounces), preferably the tender inner stalks*

5 or 6 *scallions (about 5 ounces)*

1 *small head cauliflower (about 1 pound), washed and separated into 1 1/2-inch flowerets*

6 *large radishes, washed and cut into 1/4-inch slices*

FOR THE DRESSING

2 *tablespoons Dijon-style mustard*

1/3 *cup peanut oil*

1 *tablespoon cider vinegar*

1/2 *teaspoon salt*

1/2 *teaspoon freshly ground black pepper*

1. Bring 4 cups water to a boil.

2. Meanwhile, trim and wash the zucchini. Cut them crosswise into 3-inch chunks, and then lengthwise into 1/2-inch sticks. Peel the carrots and the celery, and cut both into sticks 2 inches by 1/2 inch. Trim and wash the scallions, and cut them into 2-inch sticks.

3. Add the carrots and celery to the boiling water. Cook for 2 minutes. Add the cauliflower, boil for 5 minutes, and then add the zucchini and cook for 1 minute. Stir in the scallions and radishes and cook for 10 seconds. Drain, reserving the vegetable stock for soup.

4. *For the dressing:* Mix together the dressing ingredients in a bowl suitable for serving the salad. Add the hot vegetables and toss to coat with the dressing. Serve lukewarm or at room temperature, but not cold.

NOTE: The dressing can be doubled and the excess stored in a small jar in the refrigerator for a few weeks. Place all the dressing ingredients in the jar and shake vigorously to mix. This mustard vinaigrette is excellent on any type of green salad.

YIELD: 6 SERVINGS

MACARONI BEAUCAIRE

TOTAL TIME:
1 HOUR

This is actually two recipes incorporated into one; the elbow macaroni, which is tossed with olive oil, Parmesan cheese, seasonings, and chives,
could be served as is. Here I've expanded on it with a vegetable garnish of
thin slices of sautéed eggplant alternated with slices of tomato, layering these
vegetables underneath and on top of the macaroni to encase it, then finishing
with a coating of shredded Cheddar cheese (although grated Swiss or Parmesan cheese would be just as good). Be sure to reserve the nicest slices of
eggplant and tomato for the top of the gratin, using the less attractive slices
underneath.

1 *pound elbow macaroni*

$1/4$ *cup olive oil*

2 *tablespoons grated Parmesan cheese*

1 *teaspoon salt*

$1/2$ *teaspoon freshly ground black pepper*

$1/4$ *cup minced chives*

FOR THE VEGETABLE GARNISH

$1/2$ *cup canola oil*

2 *eggplants (about 1 $1/2$ pounds total), cut lengthwise into*
   12 slices, each about $1/2$ inch thick

$1/2$ *teaspoon salt*

3 *ripe tomatoes (about 1 pound), cut into $1/2$-inch slices*

1 *cup shredded Cheddar cheese*

1. Bring 3 quarts water to a boil in a pot. Add the macaroni, and
stir frequently until the water returns to the boil so the elbows don't stick to
the bottom of the pan.

2. Cook the macaroni until just tender, from 15 to 20 minutes (depending on the manufacturer). Remove about $3/4$ cup of the cooking liquid
and place it in a serving bowl large enough to hold the macaroni. Drain the
elbows in a colander. Add the olive oil, grated cheese, salt, and pepper to
the reserved cooking liquid in the bowl. Mix well, then add the drained
macaroni and the chives, and mix well again. Set aside.

3. *For the vegetable garnish:* Heat the canola oil in a large skillet. When hot, add the eggplant slices in one layer, sprinkle them with the salt, and sauté them for 2¹/₂ to 3 minutes on each side, until soft and nicely browned. Remove with a slotted spoon and drain on paper towels.

4. Reserve the 6 nicest slices of eggplant and half of the tomato slices, and arrange the remainder of these vegetables in a 14- by 10-inch gratin dish so they completely cover the bottom of the dish. Distribute the macaroni evenly on top, and arrange the reserved eggplant and tomato slices in an alternating pattern over the macaroni. Sprinkle with the shredded cheese. (The dish can be prepared ahead to this point and refrigerated until serving time.)

5. Place the gratin in a preheated 400-degree oven for approximately 20 minutes (25 to 30 if the dish has been refrigerated), until the cheese has melted and the macaroni is heated through. Serve immediately.

YIELD: 6 SERVINGS

Strawberry Summer Pudding

TOTAL TIME:
15 MINUTES
PLUS 2 TO 3
HOURS
REFRIGERATION

You can, of course, use other types of berries in this dessert. Make your selection based on what the season and/or your garden has to offer.

About 1 1/2 pints (1 1/4 pounds) ripe strawberries

1/2 cup sugar

6 ounces bread

3/4 cup strawberry jam

1 cup sour cream (optional)

1. Clean and hull the strawberries. Cut 12 of the berries into thin slices (you should have about 1 1/4 cups), and mix them with 2 tablespoons of the sugar. Set aside.

2. Place the bread in the bowl of a food processor and process for a few seconds to make coarse bread crumbs (you should have 2 cups). Set aside.

3. Place the whole berries, the jam, and the remaining sugar in the processor bowl, and process until smooth. Transfer to a bowl and lightly fold in the bread crumbs. Divide the pudding among six 1-cup containers. Refrigerate for at least 2 to 3 hours.

4. To serve, spoon the reserved berry slices onto six dessert dishes. Unmold the puddings on top of the berries, and serve with the sour cream, if desired.

YIELD: 6 SERVINGS

@

MENU 2.

Spaghetti with Basil Pesto
Herb-Stuffed Zucchini Boats
Honeyed Melon

When no one in my household feels like eating much—and this happens often in hot weather—we usually end up with pasta. It is quick, easy, economical, and always welcome.

Although we like it with fish and shellfish as well as meat, either in a sauce or alongside, more often than not we eat it with herbs or vegetables—ideal hot-weather fare. Fresh produce is at its best, available in all markets and reasonably priced in season.

Spaghetti with Basil Pesto would be quite costly if prepared in the winter, since it requires a lot of fresh basil and parsley. But, in full summer, basil and parsley are free if you have a garden of your own, and inexpensive to buy if you don't.

Zucchini—always abundant and inexpensive in the summer—is regularly featured at our table. One day we might have a salad of zucchini, another day fried zucchini sticks, yet another sautéed zucchini with garlic, ratatouille with tomatoes, eggplant, and zucchini, or the Herb-Stuffed Zucchini Boats featured in this menu.

continued

The melon dessert is excellent when made with a ripe, juicy, fragrant melon. I used a large, heavy, yellowish (rather than green) cantaloupe with a pleasantly fruity smell, but honeydew or muskmelon work just as well.

With this summer menu, I suggest a cold, flavorful white wine like a Riesling from Alsace or a California Sauvignon Blanc.

SPAGHETTI WITH BASIL PESTO

TOTAL TIME:
22 TO 25
MINUTES
You might want to double or triple the pesto recipe. The sauce is very good served on grilled fish or meat, as a delicious and healthful flavoring (instead of butter or sour cream) for baked potatoes, or as a topping for other pastas. It will keep for up to a week in the refrigerator. Be sure to cover it with a piece of plastic wrap, pressing it down so it touches the surface of the pesto. This will prevent the sauce from discoloring excessively; there will still be some darkening on top, but this part can be stirred into the pesto before serving.

To serve Spaghetti with Basil Pesto as a main course, double the entire recipe.

FOR THE PESTO
1/4 cup grated Parmesan cheese
1/4 cup walnuts or pecans
5 cloves garlic, peeled
1 small jalapeño pepper, cut in half and seeded (optional)
1 cup (tightly packed) parsley leaves
2 cups (moderately well packed) basil leaves
1/2 cup virgin olive oil

1 pound thin spaghetti (# 4)
1 1/2 teaspoons salt
Freshly ground black pepper to taste
Hot pepper flakes (optional)
Grated Parmesan cheese, for garnish

1. Bring about 4 quarts water to a boil in a pot.

2. *Meanwhile, for the pesto:* Place the Parmesan cheese, nuts, garlic, jalapeño pepper, if desired, parsley, and basil in the bowl of a food processor. Process for about 30 seconds, until the mixture is finely pureed. Add the oil and process a few more seconds. There should be about 1 1/2 cup. Set aside.

3. About 10 minutes before serving, add the spaghetti and 1 teaspoon of the salt to the boiling water. Return the water to a boil and boil over high heat for 8 to 9 minutes, for slightly al dente spaghetti, or longer as preferred.

4. Using a measuring cup, remove 1 cup of the cooking liquid. Mix this cooking liquid with the pesto mixture in a large bowl. Drain the pasta well in a colander and add it to the sauce with the remaining 1/2 teaspoon salt and pepper to taste. Toss and serve immediately with hot pepper flakes, if desired, and grated Parmesan cheese.

NOTE: When making a pasta dish, many cooks wait until they have finished preparing the sauce before putting water on to boil for the pasta, even though the second step usually takes longer than the first. Remember to put the pot of water on to boil when you begin making the sauce.

YIELD: 6 SERVINGS

HERB-STUFFED ZUCCHINI BOATS

TOTAL TIME:
ABOUT 2 HOURS

These stuffed zucchini can be served cold or hot. If you serve the dish cold, sharpen the flavor by garnishing it with additional fresh herbs just before serving: Fresh basil, tarragon, parsley, or chives are good choices in summer. When the weather is cooler, this dish can be made heartier with the addition of chopped leftover cooked meat or cold cuts.

6 zucchini of equal size (about 3 pounds total)

2 tablespoons virgin olive oil, plus 2 to 3 tablespoons for garnish

2 onions (about 12 ounces), peeled and coarsely chopped (about 1 1/2 cups)

4 cloves garlic, peeled, crushed, and chopped (about 1 tablespoon)

1/2 cup minced scallions (about 5 scallions)

5 cups 1-inch cubes of leftover bread

1 cup milk

1/2 cup chopped herbs (chives, parsley, or basil or a mixture of these), plus extra if serving cold

1/2 cup grated Parmesan cheese

1/8 TO 1/4 teaspoon cayenne pepper, to taste

2 large eggs

1 teaspoon salt

1/2 teaspoon freshly ground black pepper

Red wine vinegar (optional)

1. Wash the zucchini, trim the ends, and cut in half lengthwise. Using a metal measuring tablespoon with sharp edges, hollow out the inside of the zucchini; remove most of the seeds and a little of the flesh so the remaining shells are about 1/4 inch thick. There should be about 4 cups of flesh and seeds. Chop coarsely into 1/2-inch pieces, and set aside.

2. Heat the 2 tablespoons olive oil in a skillet. When hot, add the onions and sauté for 4 to 5 minutes over medium to high heat. Add the garlic, scallions, and reserved zucchini flesh and seeds and sauté for 10 to

15 seconds. Then cover and cook for 5 minutes, until the mixture is soft. Set aside.

3. Combine the bread and milk in a bowl and mash together until most of the milk has been absorbed by the bread and the mixture is like a paste. Add the chopped herbs, Parmesan cheese, cayenne, eggs, $^1/_2$ teaspoon of the salt, and the pepper. Mix well and combine with the reserved zucchini mixture.

4. Arrange the zucchini boats in a large roasting pan and sprinkle with the remaining $^1/_2$ teaspoon salt. Mound equal portions of the stuffing into the boats and place in a preheated 375-degree oven. Bake for 30 to 35 minutes.

5. Place the zucchini under a hot broiler for 4 to 5 minutes to brown the stuffing on top. Serve hot, sprinkled with the 2 to 3 tablespoons olive oil, or serve cool (not cold), sprinkled with the olive oil and additional herbs (chives, tarragon, parsley, etc.). If you prefer a more pungent taste, sprinkle a little vinegar on top before serving.

YIELD: 6 SERVINGS

HONEYED MELON

TOTAL TIME:
10 MINUTES
(PLUS CHILLING
TIME)

The most important requirement for this dessert is a ripe melon. If you can't find one, use fresh, ripe peaches or plums instead. For best results, prepare the dessert ahead and let the fruit macerate in the sauce for a few hours in the refrigerator.

1 *large ripe cantaloupe, honeydew melon, or muskmelon (about 3 pounds)*

¹/₄ *cup honey*

¹/₂ *cup orange juice*

3 *tablespoons dark rum*

1. Cut the melon in half and, using a spoon, remove the seeds. Cut each half into 4 wedges. Remove the flesh from each wedge in a single piece and cut each slice into 5 pieces. You should have a good 4 cups of melon pieces, each about 1 ¹/₂ inches square.

2. Combine the honey, orange juice, and rum in a bowl. Add the melon pieces and toss well to mix thoroughly. Cover with plastic wrap and refrigerate for several hours, or until serving time.

YIELD: 6 SERVINGS

❦

Zucchini-Yogurt Soup
Pasta Shells with Ricotta Filling
Strawberry and Orange Coupe

On hot summer nights vegetables and fruits are cooling, cleansing, refreshing, and appealing when nothing else will do. Times like these call for a vegetarian menu.

To start off, try the Zucchini-Yogurt Soup, lightly flavored with curry. It can be served either hot or cold.

Large pasta shells are good to have on hand. For this vegetarian menu, they are cooked and then stuffed with a ricotta cheese mixture, but on another occasion they could be stuffed instead with shrimp salad or ratatouille and served at room temperature as an hors d'oeuvre.

For dessert, fresh strawberries are combined with strawberry jam and orange juice to create a refreshing coupe. Julienned orange rind lends texture, color, and taste to the dessert, which is best served in stemmed wine glasses.

The soup can be made up to one day ahead and its taste will develop in the refrigerator. The pasta can be cooked and stuffed and the sauce prepared ahead, with final cooking put off until the last moment. The dessert can be prepared a few hours ahead and left to macerate until serving time.

continued

The only menu addition I might suggest would be a summer salad, perhaps featuring cucumber or watercress, to serve with the pasta. A dry white wine, a light, cool red wine, or a blush wine would go well with this meal.

ZUCCHINI-YOGURT SOUP

TOTAL TIME:
35 MINUTES The soup can be served cold or hot; if it is served hot, the yogurt must be added to each bowl just before serving, because overheating yogurt will cause it to break down.

Use another variety of squash here, if you like, and replace the apples with equal amounts of banana or pear for a different taste.

For a less-caloric soup, replace the regular yogurt with lowfat or nonfat yogurt, and dilute the stock (or replace it entirely) with water.

1^1/$_2$ *pounds zucchini (see Note)*

2   *tablespoons olive oil*

2   *onions, peeled and cut into* ^{1}/$_2$-*inch dice (about 1* ^{1}/$_2$ *cups)*

2   *large cloves garlic, peeled and crushed*

1   *teaspoon curry powder*

2   *apples (about 12 ounces), peeled, cored, and diced (about 2 cups)*

2   *cups homemade chicken stock or canned broth*

1   *teaspoon salt (or slightly more if the chicken stock is unsalted)*

^{1}/$_4$ *teaspoon Tabasco sauce*

1^1/$_2$ *cups plain yogurt*

1. Trim off and discard the ends of the zucchini. Wash the zucchini carefully under cold water and cut it into chunks about 2 inches long. Cut several ^{1}/$_4$-inch slices from the outside of the zucchini chunks, stack these slices together, and cut them into fine strips (julienne) to obtain 1 cup; set aside for a garnish. Cut the remainder of the zucchini into a 1-inch dice.

2. Heat the oil in a pot and add the onions and crushed garlic. Cook over medium heat for about 5 minutes, then add the curry powder, apples, the diced zucchini, the stock, 2 cups water, and the salt. Bring to a boil, reduce the heat to low, cover, and boil gently for 15 minutes.

3. While the soup is cooking, place the reserved julienne of zucchini and 1 cup water in a small saucepan. Bring to a boil, boil for 1 minute, and set the pan aside.

4. When the soup has cooked for 15 minutes, strain it through a sieve into a bowl. Process the solids in a food processor for about 1 minute, until very smooth, and add to the liquid in the bowl.

5. *For hot soup:* Stir the julienned zucchini with its cooking liquid into the pureed zucchini mixture. Taste for seasonings and add salt, if needed, and the Tabasco. Ladle the soup into six individual serving bowls and garnish each with 3 to 4 tablespoons of the yogurt. Serve immediately.

6. *For cold soup:* Cool the pureed zucchini mixture to lukewarm. Whisk in the yogurt until well incorporated and add the julienne of zucchini with its cooking liquid. Taste for seasonings and add salt, if needed, and the Tabasco. Refrigerate until serving time.

NOTE: For the julienne of zucchini used as a garnish in the soup, I always use thin slices cut from the outer layer of the zucchini. The green julienne cut from these slices is beautiful and firm, better as a garnish than the seedy inner flesh of the squash.

YIELD: 6 SERVINGS

PASTA SHELLS WITH
RICOTTA FILLING

TOTAL TIME:
1 HOUR AND
10 MINUTES

Count on approximately five to six of the stuffed shells per person. A few of the shells usually break in the cooking process; any broken pieces can be cut into smaller pieces and used as a soup garnish or sprinkled around the stuffed shells in the gratin dish.

12 *ounces (about 3 dozen) large pasta shells (sometimes called "food-stuffing shells")*

2 *slices firm white bread*

FOR THE FILLING

1½ *pounds ricotta cheese*

3 *eggs*

½ *cup shredded basil or parsley or a mixture of both*

⅓ *cup grated Parmesan cheese*

1 *teaspoon freshly ground black pepper*

¾ *teaspoon salt*

FOR THE SAUCE

¼ *cup virgin olive oil*

2 *cups coarsely chopped onions*

5 *cloves garlic, peeled and sliced thin (about 2 tablespoons)*

½ *teaspoon fresh thyme or ¼ teaspoon dried thyme*

4 TO 5 *medium-size very ripe tomatoes, cut into 1-inch dice (about 4 cups), or 3 cups canned tomatoes, preferably imported, with their juice*

½ *teaspoon freshly ground black pepper*

1 *teaspoon salt*

¼ *cup shredded basil, for garnish*

1. In a pot, bring about 4 quarts water to a strong boil. Add the shells and cook until tender, approximately 15 minutes. Drain and rinse briefly under cold water to stop the cooking. Set aside.

2. Place the bread slices in the bowl of a food processor. Process briefly until crumbed. You should have 1 cup of bread crumbs.

3. *For the filling:* Place the ricotta cheese, eggs, basil and/or parsley, Parmesan cheese, bread crumbs, pepper, and salt in a bowl, and mix well. Using a spoon, fill the pasta shells. (You will see that some of the pasta shells have broken into pieces during the cooking process. Cut them into small pieces and set aside.)

4. Arrange the filled shells in one or two large gratin dishes so that they touch one another but are not overlapping or crowded. Sprinkle the broken pieces of pasta around them.

5. *For the sauce:* Heat the oil in a saucepan. When it is hot, add the onions, garlic, and thyme and cook for about 2 minutes. Then add the tomatoes, 1 1/2 cups water, the pepper, and salt, and bring to a boil. Boil for about 3 to 4 minutes.

6. Spoon the sauce on top of and around the filled shells and cover with aluminum foil. Place in a preheated 400-degree oven and bake for about 20 minutes. (If the assembled dish has been allowed to cool before it is baked, add 10 to 12 minutes to the oven cooking time.) Sprinkle with shredded basil and serve.

YIELD: 6 SERVINGS

Strawberry and Orange Coupe

TOTAL TIME:
15 MINUTES
PLUS
CHILLING TIME

Other versions of this fruit dessert can be served year-round, with different fruits substituted for the strawberries. The berry mixture can be prepared a few hours ahead, but do not make it a day ahead or the fruit will get soft and mushy.

1   *quart (1 3/4 pounds) strawberries*

3 TO 4   *medium-size oranges (to yield 1 cup juice)*

1   *cup strawberry jam*

2   *tablespoons dark rum*

Mint sprigs, for garnish

1. Carefully wash the berries, and hull them. Cut the larger ones into 3 to 4 pieces and the smaller ones in half. Set aside in a serving bowl.

2. With a vegetable peeler, cut 3 or 4 strips from the outermost surface of 1 of the oranges. Stack the strips together and slice them into fine strips (julienne). You should have about 2 to 3 tablespoons. Add to the strawberries. Squeeze the juice from the oranges, and strain it. You should have 1 cup.

3. With a whisk, mix the orange juice, strawberry jam, and rum in a small bowl. Add this mixture to the strawberries, stir, and refrigerate until serving time. Serve cool (but not ice cold) in champagne or wine glasses, garnishing each serving with a sprig of mint.

YIELD: 6 SERVINGS

SUMMER PICKINGS

Tomatoes on Garlic Toasts
Cod with Olives
Peaches in Red Wine

Once tomatoes and peaches come into season, both frequently find their way into my summer menus.

Tomatoes, in one form or another, appear almost daily on my table throughout the late summer months. I serve them in salads with basil, in the Provençal manner—sautéed in oil over high heat—as well as stuffed, in tomato soup, in sauce over pasta, or in a refreshing first course with garlic croûtons.

Although I grow a few tomatoes in my garden, I buy most of what I need at farm markets. They are at their most delicious and least expensive in late July and August, and I usually freeze some for winter.

And from about the middle to the end of August I can usually find white peaches at a few local farm markets. When I have the opportunity, I pick this delicate freestone fruit from the trees myself. These peaches are so delicious that we eat them plain most of the time, although occasionally I use them in desserts, sometimes pureeing them—for sherbet or a Bellini, that wonderful Italian concoction with champagne—and sometimes poaching them in red wine, as I do here.

Cod with Olives can be made with almost any other fish steak or fillet. I am fortunate to live on the Connecticut shoreline, and in the summers can usually obtain blackfish and yellowtail flounder, as well as cod. All are fresh and inexpensive at that time of year, and I take advantage of their availability and use them interchangeably in recipes like this.

The fish is garnished with zucchini and Calamata olives, available at the delicatessen counters of most larger supermarkets. Or you can use another variety of olive—perhaps an oil-cured type from Morocco or California. Cod is a very mild flavored fish, and olives give it some added "zip."

Use a crusty baguette or country-type loaf for the Tomatoes on Garlic Toasts. I spread virgin olive oil on a cookie sheet and then press slices of the bread into the oil to coat them lightly before browning them in the oven—that way, only a small amount of oil is needed to produce a crusty toast. When the toasts emerge from the oven, garlic is rubbed on their rough-textured surfaces to give them a special taste.

With this summer menu, serve steamed potatoes or corn on the cob and a chilled white wine. There are some great bargains to be found in Chilean and Australian wines: Rosemount, from the Hunter Valley in Australia, produces a good product at a good price.

SPECIAL TIP: *Summer's tomato bounty can be frozen for winter use. To freeze tomatoes, cut them in half, press out the seeds and juice, and seal in plastic bags before placing them in the freezer. When you defrost them, the skin will slide off, leaving you with delicious tomato pulp to use in winter soups and sauces.*

TOMATOES ON GARLIC TOASTS

Prepare this dish about half an hour ahead of serving time so the toast can absorb the flavor of the tomato and soften up a bit. (The tomato mixture also makes a delicious pasta sauce.)

TOTAL TIME:
20 MINUTES PLUS
20 TO 30 MINUTES
SITTING TIME

1 *baguette, about 2¹/₂ inches in diameter and weighing about 8 ounces*

¹/₃ *cup virgin olive oil, plus extra for sprinkling*

1 *large clove garlic, peeled*

2 *ripe tomatoes (about 1¹/₄ pounds), seeded and cut into ¹/₂-inch dice (about 3 cups)*

5 *scallions, cleaned and minced fine (about ¹/₂ cup)*

1 *small onion (about 2 ounces), halved and thinly sliced (about ¹/₂ cup)*

¹/₂ *cup minced herbs (a mixture of chives, oregano, and parsley)*

1 *tablespoon red wine vinegar*

³/₄ *teaspoon salt*

¹/₂ *teaspoon freshly ground black pepper*

1. Cut the baguette into 24 slices, each about ¹/₂ inch thick. Spread 2 tablespoons of the olive oil on a rimmed cookie sheet and press the bread slices, first one side and then the other, into the oil. Arrange the slices in a single layer on the cookie sheet and bake in a preheated 400-degree oven for 10 minutes, until nicely browned and crusty.

2. When the toast slices are cool enough to handle, rub them lightly on both sides with the peeled garlic glove. Set aside.

3. Combine the tomatoes, scallions, onions, herbs, the remaining olive oil, the vinegar, salt, and pepper in a bowl. Set aside.

4. About 20 to 30 minutes before serving, arrange 4 toast slices on each plate and spoon the tomato mixture on top.

5. Sprinkle a little olive oil around and on top of the rounds before serving.

YIELD: 6 SERVINGS

COD WITH OLIVES

TOTAL TIME:
18 MINUTES

You can substitute almost any other fish steak or fillet for the cod. Be sure, however, to take the thickness of fish into account when determining the cooking time. If your steaks are thicker or thinner than mine (an inch), reduce or increase the cooking time accordingly. A small yellowtail sole fillet, for example, is much thinner and so will take only one minute per side to cook.

2 *pounds thick cod fillets, cut into 6 steaks about 1 inch thick and weighing 5 to 6 ounces each*

¼ *teaspoon salt*

¼ *teaspoon freshly ground black pepper*

2 *tablespoons vegetable oil*

2 *tablespoons unsalted butter*

1 *cup diced (¼-inch) zucchini (4 ounces)*

1 *cup diced (¼-inch) Calamata olives*

1. Sprinkle the cod steaks with the salt and pepper. Divide the oil and butter equally between two nonstick skillets and place over medium to high heat. When hot, sauté the cod for about 3 minutes on each side (or more or less if your steaks are thicker or thinner than 1 inch). Transfer the steaks to a platter and set them aside in a warm place.

2. Sauté the zucchini for 1 minute in the drippings in the skillet. Add the olives and sauté for another minute. Spoon over the cod and serve immediately.

YIELD: 6 SERVINGS

PEACHES IN RED WINE

The peaches are sweetened with sugar and some crème de cassis (black currant syrup) or crème de mûre (blackberry syrup). I steep them in a Pinot Noir, which works quite well in this context, but any robust red wine can be used. If you are unable to find white peaches, substitute another variety of ripe peach. Serve this attractive dessert in wine glasses or glass dishes.

TOTAL TIME: 15 MINUTES PLUS 1 HOUR REFRIGERATION

6 *ripe peaches (preferably white), about 6 ounces each*
1 *cup red wine (Pinot Noir or other robust red wine)*
¼ *cup crème de cassis (black currant syrup) or crème de mûre (blackberry syrup)*
2 *tablespoons sugar*
6 *sprigs mint, for garnish*

1. Peel the peaches and cut them into ³/4-inch wedges. Combine them in a bowl with the wine, crème de cassis, and sugar. Macerate, refrigerated, for 1 hour.

2. Spoon into glass goblets or dessert dishes and garnish with the mint. Serve.

YIELD: 6 SERVINGS

◉

Baked Chicken with Herb Crumbs
Tomatoes Provençal
Rhubarb Compote with Sour Cream

◉

Tomatoes with Chicken Stuffing

Here is another menu that takes full advantage of tomatoes and fresh herbs, two of summer's finest bonuses. Although chicken parts can be used in the Baked Chicken with Herb Crumbs, whole chickens are cheaper. The skin of the chickens should be removed because it won't brown well under the coating of bread crumbs and fresh herbs. It pulls away easily, leaving a less fatty, though still moist, chicken.

Tomatoes Provençal is a classic dish, simple and delicious when the tomatoes are fleshy and ripe. They are flavored with a mixture of chopped parsley and chopped garlic—called *persillade* in French—which is a signature of the cooking of Provence.

The tomato halves are first seared, cut side down, in a very hot skillet, then placed on a serving plate or in a gratin dish and sprinkled with the *persillade* and olive oil, and finally warmed for a few minutes in the oven.

I love stewed rhubarb, preferring it not overly sweetened, so the natural sour taste is still dominant. Sometimes I use rhubarb in open-face pies; at other times I enclose it in dough. The compote in this menu is served with sour cream and, if you desire, cookies or pound cake.

The Tomatoes with Chicken Stuffing are made with leftover chicken and, if there are any, leftover Tomatoes Provençal. Other leftover roast meat can be used to supplement the chicken.

This summer menu might start with Beet Salad (page 72) or a cucumber salad. A chilled white wine would go well with the meal. The Tomatoes with Chicken Stuffing can be served alone for lunch or with a pasta dish for dinner the next day.

BAKED CHICKEN WITH HERB CRUMBS

TOTAL TIME:
ABOUT 1 HOUR

Use fresh bread crumbs if at all possible for this dish. If you must use dried crumbs, use only half the amount called for in the recipe.

The wing tips can be cut off the chickens and frozen along with the necks and gizzards for later use in stock, and the livers can be sautéed briefly and served with aperitifs or enjoyed while you are cooking.

The chickens can be prepared in advance to the point where they are macerated with the olive oil, Tabasco, and salt. The herb coating can also be prepared ahead but should not be put on the chickens until you are ready to cook them.

2 *3¹/₂-pound chickens*

3 *tablespoons olive oil or vegetable oil*

¹/₄ *teaspoon Tabasco sauce*

¹/₄ *teaspoon salt*

5 *slices firm white bread (to yield about 2¹/₂ cups fresh bread crumbs) (see Special Tip, page 243)*

2 *sprigs fresh thyme or ¹/₂ teaspoon dried thyme*

2 *sprigs fresh oregano or ¹/₂ teaspoon dried oregano*

¹/₄ *cup chopped chives or parsley*

¹/₂ *teaspoon freshly ground black pepper*

1. Cut off the wing tips of the chickens and set aside with the necks and gizzards. (These can be wrapped and frozen for future use in stock or soup.) Holding 1 chicken on its side, cut through the backbone, beginning at the neck end, with a sharp knife. Spread the chicken open, lay it bone side down on the table, and press it against the table with your hands to flatten it. Pull off the skin; it should come off easily except, perhaps, around the wings. Remove as much as you can. Repeat with the other chicken. (See Note.)

2. Place the 2 chickens flesh side up on a jelly-roll pan and rub them with 1 tablespoon of the oil and the Tabasco. Sprinkle with the salt. Cover and refrigerate until ready to cook.

3. Prepare the herb coating: Put the bread slices in the bowl of a food processor, and process to crumbs. If using fresh thyme and fresh oregano, chop the leaves in a food processor, mini-chop, or by hand with a sharp knife. Combine the bread crumbs, thyme, oregano, parsley, pepper, and the remaining 2 tablespoons oil. Toss gently to coat the bread crumbs lightly with the oil.

4. When ready to cook, pat the herb coating lightly over the surface of the chickens. Place them in a preheated 400-degree oven, and bake for 30 to 35 minutes, until the chicken is cooked through and the crumbs are nicely browned. Remove and let sit for 10 minutes. Cut into pieces and serve.

NOTE: The skin of the chicken can be used to make crackling to crumble on an accompanying salad. Spread the skin smooth, outer side up, on a cookie sheet and sprinkle it with salt. Roast in a 400-degree oven for about 20 to 25 minutes, until crisp.

YIELD: 6 SERVINGS

TOMATOES PROVENÇAL

TOTAL TIME:

15 MINUTES

If there are any leftovers from this classic dish from the south of France, they can be chopped and added to the sauce for the Tomatoes with Chicken Stuffing.

6   *very ripe tomatoes (about 2¹/₂ pounds total, 6 to 7 ounces each)*
1   *cup lightly packed parsley leaves*
4   *cloves garlic, peeled and crushed*
¹/₄ *cup olive oil or vegetable oil*
¹/₂ *teaspoon freshly ground black pepper*
¹/₂ *teaspoon salt*

1. Remove and discard the stems from the tomatoes and cut them in half crosswise. Chop the parsley and garlic together to make a *persillade*. There should be ¹/₂ cup.

2. In each of two heavy skillets heat about 1 tablespoon of the oil until very hot. Place the tomatoes cut side down in the skillets, and cook them over high heat for about 2 minutes, covered, until the tomatoes soften slightly. Arrange the tomatoes cut side up in a gratin dish suitable for serving. Sprinkle with the pepper and salt.

3. Add the remaining oil and the *persillade* to the drippings in the pan. Stir over the heat for 10 to 15 seconds to cook slightly, and then divide the mixture equally among the tomatoes, spreading it over the tops. Put the tomatoes in a warm oven (250 degrees) for a few minutes before serving. If the tomatoes must sit 30 minutes or more before being served, sauté them as directed and keep warm in a 180-degree oven, but don't add the *persillade* until serving time.

YIELD: 6 SERVINGS

RHUBARB COMPOTE WITH SOUR CREAM

Rhubarb is a good vehicle for using leftover preserves, jellies, or jams that have collected in the refrigerator. This recipe calls for one and a half cups of jam, which can be mixed from jellies as varied as orange, apricot, and currant.

TOTAL TIME: 25 MINUTES

2 *pounds ripe, red rhubarb ribs*
$^1/_2$ *cup apple cider or orange juice*
1$^1/_2$ *cups jam, jelly, or preserves*
1 *cup sour cream*
Pound cake or cookies (optional)

1. Wash the rhubarb ribs and trim off and discard any leaves or imperfections. Cut the ribs into pieces 2 to 3 inches long, splitting the larger ribs in half before cutting them into pieces.

2. Put the ribs in a saucepan with the cider and jam. Cover and bring to a boil over high heat. Reduce the heat and boil gently for about 5 minutes; then remove the cover and continue boiling for about 10 minutes. The rhubarb will shred into pieces. Cool and transfer to a serving bowl.

3. Serve with a dollop of the sour cream and, if desired, pound cake or cookies.

YIELD: 6 SERVINGS

TOMATOES WITH CHICKEN STUFFING

TOTAL TIME:
1 HOUR AND 25
MINUTES

I cut a "cap" from each tomato at the stem end to make a nice "hat" for the stuffed tomatoes. The tomatoes are hollowed out with a measuring spoon, which has a fairly sharp edge. Don't worry if you aren't able to remove all the interior flesh, seeds, and juice.

If you do not have enough leftover chicken, leftover roast pork, beef, or veal will work equally well; or simply increase the other ingredients — from the bread to the milk and the eggs — to compensate. Pieces of ham or even sandwich meat can be chopped and added as well to extend the filling mixture.

6   *very ripe tomatoes (about 2¹/₂ pounds total, 6 to 7 ounces each)*

FOR THE STUFFING

3   *slices bread*

¹/₂   *cup milk*

1   *large egg*

³/₄   *teaspoon freshly ground black pepper*

1   *teaspoon salt*

³/₄   *cup chopped onion (1 medium-size onion)*

2 TO 3   *cloves garlic, crushed and chopped (about 1¹/₂ teaspoons)*

3   *tablespoons chopped parsley*

2   *cups diced leftover chicken from Baked Chicken with Herb Crumbs (page 108)*

FOR THE SAUCE

2   *tablespoons olive oil*

3   *cloves garlic, peeled and sliced thin*

¹/₂   *teaspoon sugar*

Dash cayenne pepper

1. Cut off the very top of each tomato at the stem end to create a ¼-inch lid. Set aside. Using a measuring spoon, scoop out the insides of the tomatoes and place in a bowl. Gently squeeze the tomatoes to loosen any remaining juice and seeds and add to the contents of the bowl. Coarsely chop or process the juice, seeds, and pulp briefly in a food processor and set aside for use in the sauce. You should have about 2 cups.

2. *For the stuffing:* Mix the bread and milk together in a bowl, mashing the bread with your fingers to help it absorb the milk. Stir in the egg, ½ teaspoon of the pepper, and ½ teaspoon of the salt. Add the onion, chopped garlic, parsley, and chicken; mix gently to combine. Stuff the tomatoes evenly with the stuffing mixture, mounding it on top. Set the little lids on top of each filled tomato.

3. *For the sauce:* Pour the reserved chopped tomato mixture into a gratin dish. Stir in the olive oil, sliced garlic, sugar, the remaining ¼ teaspoon pepper, the cayenne, the remaining ½ teaspoon salt, and ½ cup water.

4. Arrange the stuffed tomatoes on top of the sauce, place in a preheated 375-degree oven, and bake for about 1 hour, until tender and cooked through. Serve immediately, or set aside and serve later at room temperature.

YIELD: 6 SERVINGS

TWO SUPPERS FROM THE GRILL

MENU 1.

Hot or Cold Leek Soup
Haddock on Polenta
Grilled Turkey Wings

Soup is almost always on our menus at home. In the summer, the sturdy winter varieties are replaced by light vegetable or fruit soups, some of which—like the leek soup in this menu—can be served cold. It is also a time when grilled food is often part of our daily fare, both because we like the way it tastes and because grilling keeps the heat of summer cooking outdoors, leaving the inside of the house much cooler.

In this very eclectic menu, there are two leek soup variations: the soup can be served hot either on its own or with croutons, or, if you have some soup left over or are looking for a good cold beginning to a hot weather meal, it can be transformed into a classic vichyssoise with the addition of a little milk or cream, chives, and Tabasco sauce.

The Haddock on Polenta makes an ideal first course for an elegant, sophisticated dinner party as well as a great main course for a family meal. The fish is simply poached in a little dry white wine and served on polenta with a tarragon-flavored sauce made from the poaching liquid.

continued

Although we often buy chicken to grill outside, we also try to take advantage of some of the good buys on other varieties of poultry at the market. In addition to seeking out large family-size packages of chicken wings or drumsticks for grilling, I look for Cornish hens as well. And for this menu, I have transformed large, meaty, inexpensive turkey wings into a delicious grilled edible. The sauce is much lighter than a conventional ketchup or barbecue sauce; made with vinegar, dark soy sauce, garlic, and spices, it coats the meat lightly enough so that it can brown naturally, and it has a wonderful flavor.

You may in fact want to make two separate meals from the dishes featured in this menu—the hot leek soup followed by the haddock one day, and the cold vichyssoise followed by the turkey wings another day. A salad always goes well, and for dessert, fruit would be the perfect choice, although no one can argue with ice cream on a hot summer night.

With this exciting summer menu, a good-quality, reasonably priced, chilled white wine from the state of Washington—like a Chateau Ste. Michelle—would be a good choice.

Hot or Cold Leek Soup

TOTAL TIME:
45 MINUTES
PLUS COOLING
TIME FOR COLD
SOUP

If you cannot find leeks, add additional onions or scallions; the soup will be very good, although it won't have the unique taste that leeks give to soup. If using leeks or scallions, be sure to make use of the green as well as the white part of the vegetables, after trimming them first, of course, to eliminate any damaged or wilted sections. The green leaves lend color as well as taste and texture to the soup.

1 *large leek (about 8 ounces)*

2 *tablespoons olive oil*

1 *onion (about 6 ounces), peeled and sliced*

6 *cups chicken stock*

1¹/₂ *pounds potatoes, peeled and cut into 2-inch pieces*

Salt to taste (depending on the saltiness of the stock)

¹/₂ *teaspoon freshly ground black pepper*

Bread croutons, for garnish (optional)

2¹/₂ *cups cold milk*

6 *tablespoons chopped chives*

¹/₄ *teaspoon Tabasco sauce*

1. Remove the root end and any damaged outer leaves from the leek,
but leave the remainder of the leaves intact. Split the leek in half lengthwise,
and cut it into ¹/₂-inch pieces. Clean the leek by immersing the pieces in a
bowl filled with cold water. Lift the pieces from the water and place them
in a sieve to drain.

2. Heat the oil in a pot. When hot, add the leek and sliced onion,
and cook over medium heat for about 5 minutes, until they soften and begin
to brown lightly. Add the stock, potatoes, salt, and pepper, and bring to
the boil. Boil for 30 to 40 minutes, until the potatoes are tender.

3. Strain off most of the cooking juices and reserve them. Add the
solids with a little of the juices to the bowl of a food processor, and process
briefly, just until pureed. (If too much liquid is added to the processor bowl,
the mixture will become too foamy.) Stir the puree into the reserved juices.
You should have about 7 cups. The hot soup can be served immediately,
either plain or with croutons.

4. *For cold soup:* Cool the soup and stir in the milk, chives, and
Tabasco sauce. Serve cold.

YIELD: 6 SERVINGS

HADDOCK ON POLENTA

TOTAL TIME:
45 MINUTES
You don't have to limit yourself to haddock for this recipe — select the freshest, most economical fish you can find. The polenta is delicious on its own with roasts, as well as with any kind of poultry or stew. And, of course, the poached haddock can be served on its own, without the polenta.

1 *tablespoon unsalted butter*

$^1/_2$ *cup finely minced scallions*

6 *thick haddock fillets, each about 1 inch thick, if possible (see below), and weighing 6 to 7 ounces*

$^3/_4$ *teaspoon salt*

$^1/_2$ *teaspoon freshly ground black pepper*

1 *cup dry, fruity white wine*

$^3/_4$ *cup heavy cream*

$^3/_4$ *teaspoon potato starch dissolved in 1 tablespoon water*

1 *tablespoon chopped tarragon*

1 *tablespoon chopped chives*

Polenta (recipe follows)

1. Rub the bottom of a large saucepan with the butter. Add the scallions and the fish (fold the fillets in half if they are long and thin to approximate the thickness called for here so they will cook in about the same length of time). Add $^1/_2$ teaspoon of the salt, the pepper, and wine. Bring to a boil over high heat, cover, reduce the heat to low, and boil gently for 3 minutes.

2. Holding the lid slightly ajar on the pan so the fish don't fall out, pour the cooking juices into another saucepan. Add the cream to the juices, stir in the remaining $^1/_4$ teaspoon salt, and bring the mixture to a boil. Boil for 1 minute, add the dissolved potato starch, and return to the boil. Remove from the heat, and stir in the tarragon and chives.

3. To serve, spoon the polenta onto six individual plates. Arrange a fish fillet on top of the polenta, and spoon some tarragon sauce on top.

YIELD: 6 SERVINGS

POLENTA

1   *teaspoon salt*

1¼ *cups (6 ounces) yellow cornmeal*

TOTAL TIME:
25 TO 30 MINUTES

1. Bring a quart of water to a boil in a large saucepan and add the salt. Slowly add the cornmeal to the boiling water, sprinkling it on top of the water as you stir it in with a whisk to keep it from becoming lumpy. Cook, stirring occasionally, for 20 to 25 minutes, until thickened.

2. Serve with the haddock.

YIELD: 6 SERVINGS

GRILLED TURKEY WINGS

The turkey wings are boiled before they are grilled; they are fairly large and would take so long to grill otherwise that they would tend to dry out or the grilling sauce would burn. Boiling them briefly ahead produces a more moist, flavorful result. The sauce can also be used with great success on other grilled meats or poultry.

TOTAL TIME:
1 HOUR

6   *whole turkey wings, each with 3 sections (about 4 pounds total)*

FOR THE GRILLING SAUCE

¼   *cup red wine vinegar*

2   *tablespoons dark soy sauce*

1½ *tablespoons light brown sugar*

¾   *teaspoon dried thyme*

1   *teaspoon crushed fennel seeds*

1   *teaspoon Tabasco sauce*

3   *cloves garlic, peeled, crushed, and finely chopped (about 2 teaspoons)*

2   *scallions, cleaned and finely chopped (about 3 tablespoons)*

continued

1. Place the turkey wings in a pot, cover with 2 quarts water, and bring to a boil. Cover the pan with a lid and boil the wings gently for 15 minutes. Then set them aside in the broth until ready to grill.

2. *For the grilling sauce:* Mix together all the sauce ingredients in a bowl. Set aside.

3. When ready to grill, remove the wings from the broth (freeze this turkey stock for future use in a soup or stew), place them, meaty side up, on a grill (preferably with a cover) over medium-high to high heat, cover, and grill for about 12 minutes. Turn the wings over (the underside should be nicely browned) and brush them with the sauce. Grill, covered, for another 12 minutes. Turn again, brush with the sauce, and grill for another 5 minutes. The wings should be well browned on all sides.

4. Arrange the wings on a serving platter, brush with the remaining grilling sauce, and either serve immediately or cool to lukewarm before serving.

YIELD: 6 SERVINGS

SPECIAL TIP   GRILLED SPARERIBS: *Substitute pork spareribs for the turkey wings and prepare them as indicated in the recipe, first boiling them gently for 30 minutes and then finishing them on the grill in the same manner and for the same length of time as the turkey wings.*

@

Flan of Green Herbs
Spicy Grilled Beef Roast
Swiss Chard Gratin

I built a stone-and-cement barbecue pit years ago and make wood-burning fires in it occasionally to cook for large outdoor parties. But for everyday use and small gatherings, I use a hooded gas grill with a burner on the side that is on my back porch. There is a casualness and freedom out of doors that is compatible with straightforward summer fare.

Use either wood charcoal or gas for grilling. Conventional briquets, a petroleum derivative, can impart an unpleasant flavor and present a possible health hazard if not used properly. If you must use them, be sure they have burned until they are white and have stopped smoking before putting the meat or other food on to grill.

The Flan of Green Herbs in this menu is a variation on a fines herbes omelet recipe. This version, using only four eggs for six people instead of the usual three eggs per person, is less caloric and has far less cholesterol. It is served lukewarm or at room temperature and makes use of every herb in my garden. For six servings, it contains—in addition to four cups of spinach—a loosely packed six-cup mixture of sorrel, cilantro, parsley, chervil, chives, basil, tarragon, oregano, and arugula.

The sauce served with the flan is a refreshing puree of raw tomatoes flavored with a little olive oil and vinegar. It is equally good served over poached fish or mixed with pasta.

The Spicy Grilled Beef Roast came about as the result of my search for less expensive main dishes. For this recipe, you can use a piece of chuck eye roast or a shoulder underblade roast (part of the same chuck and shoulder area). Although both of these cuts can be braised or roasted indoors, they are juicy and tender when grilled and much less expensive than top round, sirloin tip, or shell.

The Swiss Chard Gratin is made with young chard, so both the ribs and leaves can be used. These thin tender ribs don't require peeling like the more mature, thicker ribs available later in the season.

Add a glass of cold Côtes de Provence rosé or Tavel wine to this lovely summer meal, and finish it off with a seasonal fruit—cherries perhaps—for dessert.

FLAN OF GREEN HERBS

The mixture of herbs and greens in this recipe can be altered; bear in mind, though, that certain herbs—tarragon, basil, and cilantro, for example—have a stronger flavor and so should be used in smaller quantities than milder herbs like parsley or chervil.

TOTAL TIME: ABOUT 25 MINUTES

FOR THE FLAN

6 cups (lightly packed) mixed herbs and greens (sorrel, cilantro, parsley, chervil, chives, basil, tarragon, oregano, and/or arugula)

4 cups (lightly packed) spinach leaves

1 tablespoon unsalted butter

2 tablespoons olive oil

1 small leek, trimmed, thoroughly washed, and coarsely chopped (about 1 1/2 cups)

1/4 cup pignoli nuts

4 large eggs

1/4 cup milk

1/2 teaspoon salt

1/4 teaspoon freshly ground black pepper

FOR THE TOMATO SAUCE

2 pounds ripe tomatoes (about 4), peeled, seeded, and chopped fine in a food processor (about 2 1/2 cups)

1 tablespoon finely chopped jalapeño pepper (optional)

1 teaspoon salt

1/2 teaspoon freshly ground black pepper

1 1/2 tablespoons vinegar

1/4 cup olive oil

1. *For the flan:* Wash the herbs, greens, and spinach thoroughly and drain well. Chop coarsely.

2. Melt the butter with the olive oil in a large ovenproof stainless steel saucepan. Add the leek and sauté over medium to high heat for

2 minutes. Add the nuts and continue sautéeing for another minute. Stir in the herbs and spinach and cook for 3 minutes, until the herbs and greens are soft and tender.

3. Break the eggs into a bowl and whisk with the milk until blended. Add the mixture to the saucepan with the salt and pepper and cook, stirring, for about 15 seconds, until semisolid. Bake in a preheated 375-degree oven for 10 minutes.

4. *Meanwhile, for the tomato sauce:* Mix the tomatoes, jalapeño, salt, pepper, vinegar, and olive oil in a bowl. Set aside until serving time.

5. Cut the hot flan into wedges and serve with the sauce.

YIELD: 6 SERVINGS.

SPICY GRILLED BEEF ROAST

This small roast is actually a large steak that you carve on the bias into very thin slices. If you don't have access to a barbecue grill, the meat can be cooked in a skillet. Brown it on top of the stove over high heat for about 1 1/2 minutes on each side, and then place it in a preheated 425-degree oven for about 15 minutes to cook a 1 1/2-inch-thick steak medium rare (adjust time if the meat is thicker or thinner).

Cold leftover roast is excellent for sandwiches. Slice the beef thin and serve it layered with hot mustard, iceberg lettuce, and tomatoes between slices of toasted bread.

TOTAL TIME: ABOUT 25 MINUTES

1   *teaspoon dried rosemary*

1   *teaspoon dried oregano*

1/4   *teaspoon cayenne pepper*

1/2   *teaspoon salt*

1   *2-pound beef roast or large steak (chuck eye or shoulder underblade), 1 1/2 inches thick*

1. Mix together the rosemary, oregano, pepper, and salt in a small bowl, crushing the rosemary with your fingers as you mix. Spread the seasoning mixture on both sides of the roast.

2. Place the roast on a hot charcoal or gas grill about 8 to 10 inches from the heat and cook, covered, for about 8 minutes on each side for medium-rare meat.

3. Transfer the meat to a platter and let rest in a warm place for 10 minutes before carving. To serve, cut on the bias into very thin slices. Arrange on individual plates and serve with the Swiss Chard Gratin.

YIELD: 6 SERVINGS

Swiss Chard Gratin

TOTAL TIME:

30 MINUTES

If young green Swiss chard is not available, use bright red Swiss chard. Both are good in gratins like this one, or sautéed with oil and garlic.

1½ *pounds young (2-inch-wide ribs) Swiss chard, ribs and leaves cut into 2-inch pieces and thoroughly washed*

1 *cup grated Swiss cheese*

½ *teaspoon salt*

¼ *teaspoon freshly ground black pepper*

3 *tablespoons olive oil*

1. Bring ½ inch of water to a boil in a large saucepan. Add the Swiss chard, cover, and bring back to the boil. Boil for 5 to 6 minutes, until tender. Most of the moisture will have evaporated. (Or place the chard in 2 plastic bags and cook each bag in a microwave oven for 5 minutes. Drain.)

2. Place the Swiss chard in a gratin dish and mix in the cheese, salt, pepper, and olive oil. (The recipe can be prepared to this point a few hours ahead.)

3. When ready to cook, place the dish in a preheated 375-degree oven and bake for 15 minutes. Serve with the grilled beef.

YIELD: 6 SERVINGS

RUSSIAN CLASSIC, UPDATED

Tomato Salad with Red Onion and Basil
Salmon and Green Beans Pojarski
Parsley Potatoes

Although salmon is available year-round now because of the farm-raised Norwegian and Canadian varieties, it is at its best and least expensive during the summer, when wild salmon from the Pacific is available. This is the time to take advantage of this versatile and reliable fish.

An interesting way to enjoy it is in *pojarski*—patties of ground fish, meat, or poultry enriched with cream and eggs. Traditionally, Salmon Pojarski is made with salmon, heavy cream, and eggs processed into a tight puree. In this recipe, the needed moisture is provided by finely chopped, uncooked, fresh green beans, a combination typical of Laos and Thailand.

Instead of a conventional butter and cream sauce, the salmon is served with a hot sauce of diced cucumber, vinegar, oil, scallions, and soy sauce. It has a sharp, flavorful taste that goes well with the *pojarski*, but will also complement poached or steamed fish, as well as boiled or steamed broccoli or cauliflower.

The Tomato Salad with Red Onion and Basil is at its best in full summer when all of the ingredients are in season. Short of your own garden, local farms are the best source.

Parsley Potatoes complete the menu. Although an additional green vegetable could be served with the salmon, it is not really necessary since almost half of the salmon mixture is green beans.

An ice cream or sherbet, and a robust, well-defined white wine, like a Chardonnay from California or from Hunter Valley in Australia, would round out the meal.

TOMATO SALAD WITH RED ONION AND BASIL

You'll find that using ingredients of superior quality makes an extraordinary difference in the taste of this simple dish. Leftover salad can be enjoyed on its own or as an addition to sandwiches containing meat or poultry.

TOTAL TIME: 10 TO 12 MINUTES

4 *large ripe tomatoes (about 1 1/2 to 2 pounds)*

1 *large red onion, peeled*

1 *teaspoon salt*

3/4 *teaspoon freshly ground black pepper*

2 *tablespoons red wine vinegar*

5 *tablespoons olive oil or a mixture of olive oil and safflower, corn, or canola oil*

1/4 *cup shredded basil*

1. Cut the tomatoes crosswise into 1/4-inch slices. (Remember that a sharp blade is required to slice very ripe tomatoes.) Arrange the slices, overlapping them slightly, in a large oval or round gratin dish.

2. Cut the peeled onion into 1/8-inch-thick slices. Separate the slices into rings and arrange them over the tomatoes. Sprinkle with the salt, pepper, vinegar, and oil, coating the vegetables as evenly as possible. Sprinkle the shredded basil on top and serve at room temperature. This goes well with a crunchy, crusty French bread.

YIELD: 6 SERVINGS

SALMON AND
GREEN BEANS POJARSKI

TOTAL TIME:
35 TO 40
MINUTES

Chopped beans are mixed with the salmon along with bread crumbs, eggs, and herbs, which essentially doubles the yield of the fish. Extending the salmon in this way cuts down considerably on the price of the dish and the resulting *pojarski* are moist and flavorful. If salmon is not available, the dish can also be made with codfish, catfish, or red snapper, depending on availability and price.

The salmon mixture may be made and shaped into patties a day ahead, refrigerated, and then cooked at the last moment. The sauce can also be made ahead. The tomato salad is best when made within an hour of serving, and the potatoes should be cooked as close to eating time as possible.

About 1 3/4 pounds salmon (to accommodate trimming and removal of skin; you should have 1 1/2 pounds cleaned flesh)

10 *ounces fresh green beans*

2 *teaspoons diced (1/8 inch) jalapeño pepper (ribs and seeds removed)*

3 *large eggs*

1 1/2 *cups fresh bread crumbs (made from 3 to 4 slices fresh bread; see Note) or 3/4 cup dry bread crumbs*

3 *cloves garlic, peeled, crushed, and chopped fine (about 3/4 teaspoon)*

1/2 *teaspoon freshly ground black pepper*

1 1/2 *teaspoons salt*

1/3 *cup shredded basil*

FOR THE CUCUMBER HOT SAUCE

1 *large cucumber (about 12 ounces), preferably the "seedless" English variety*

1 *teaspoon salt*

1 *tablespoon sugar*

1/4 *teaspoon red pepper flakes (or more or less, to taste)*

3 *tablespoons cider vinegar*

1/3 *cup canola or corn oil*

2   *teaspoons soy sauce*

3   *scallions, cleaned and finely minced (about $^1/_3$ cup)*

$^1/_4$ *cup corn, safflower, or canola oil*

1. Remove and discard any skin and sinew from the salmon and cut the flesh into 1-inch pieces.

2. Cut away and discard any damaged spots on the beans, wash thoroughly in cold water, and cut into 1-inch pieces.

3. Place the green beans and jalapeño pepper in the bowl of a food processor and process until finely chopped; the mixture should be rather coarse, not smooth and liquid. You should have about 2 cups. Transfer to a bowl and set aside.

4. Place the salmon in the unwashed processor bowl and process for a few seconds, starting and stopping the machine, until coarsely chopped. Add to the bean mixture with the eggs, bread crumbs, garlic, pepper, salt, and shredded basil. Mix well.

5. Using a spoon, make 12 patties about 1 inch thick and about 3 inches across (about 3 to $3^1/_2$ ounces each). Wet your hands to keep them from sticking to the salmon mixture and arrange the patties on a tray lined with plastic wrap. Set aside while you make the sauce.

6. *For the sauce:* Peel the cucumber with a vegetable peeler and cut it in half lengthwise. With a spoon, remove the seeds. Cut the cucumber lengthwise into thin strips, and then cut the strips crosswise into a small dice. You should have about $1^1/_4$ cups.

7. Combine the cucumber with the salt, sugar, red pepper flakes, vinegar, oil, soy sauce, scallions, and $^1/_2$ cup water. Set aside until serving time.

8. To cook the salmon, use two large skillets, preferably nonstick. Heat 2 tablespoons of the oil in each skillet. When hot, add the patties and cook over medium to high heat for $2^1/_2$ minutes on each side. Set aside for a few minutes before serving.

9. To serve, arrange 2 salmon patties on each individual plate and spoon the potatoes around them. Serve the cucumber hot sauce on the side.

continued

NOTE: To make fresh bread crumbs, break fresh bread into pieces and grind in the bowl of a food processor (see Secial Tip, page 243). I prefer fresh bread crumbs to dry bread crumbs for this recipe because they are lighter and more delicate. If, however, fresh crumbs are not available, use half the amount of dry crumbs.

YIELD: 6 SERVINGS

PARSLEY POTATOES

TOTAL TIME:
32 TO 35
MINUTES

Both red and white new potatoes are plentiful and very flavorful in full summer. Remember that potatoes, whether peeled or unpeeled, must be of nearly equal size to cook properly. Trim them, if necessary, to achieve this uniformity, and then round off the cut edges to make them look more natural.

Restaurants commonly make the mistake of boiling potatoes in advance and then keeping them in water for hours before serving. For best results, drain the potatoes immediately after they are boiled or steamed and place them back on the stove for a minute or so to eliminate any moisture. Then toss them with the parsley and butter and serve.

2½ *pounds small new potatoes, peeled and cut, if necessary, into equal-size pieces (about 3 to 4 potatoes per person)*

½ *teaspoon salt*

2 *tablespoons chopped parsley or other herbs such as basil or tarragon*

2 *tablespoons unsalted butter*

1. Place the potatoes in a saucepan with cold water to cover, and add the salt. Bring to a boil, reduce the heat, and cook, covered, until tender, about 20 minutes. Drain and return to the heat for 1 minute to dry. Toss with the parsley and butter.

2. Serve with the Salmon Pojarski.

YIELD: 6 SERVINGS

Fall

SUMMER'S LEGACY

Corn Tempura
Zucchini-Tomato Gratin
Grilled Thyme Pork Chops

EASING INTO AUTUMN

Cold Zucchini Terrine
Lamb Chops Champvallon
Bread and Banana Pudding

SEPTEMBER'S RICHES

Corn Salad
Vegetable and Pasta Stew
Grilled Tuna Belly

SPECIALTIES OF THE SOUTH OF FRANCE

Pissaladière Baguettes
Brandade de Morue au Gratin
Zucchini Salad

AUTUMN'S CATCH

MENU 1.
Broiled Piquant Bluefish
Puree of Onions
Cooked Grapes with Cream

MENU 2.
Fromage Fort
Fish and Pasta with Wine Sauce
Sautéed Napa Cabbage

TWO MEALS FROM ONE SAVORY PORK ROAST

Cabbage and Basil Salad
Corn off the Cob
Braised Pork Roast with Sweet Potatoes
ↄ
Pork and Potato Hash

COLD WEATHER WARM-UP

Fiery Chili with Red Beans
Boiled Rice
Apple Fritters

TURKEY AND CRANBERRIES: A NEW LOOK

Turkey Cutlets in Anchovy-Lemon Sauce
Gratin of Butternut Squash
Cranberry Kisel

SUMMER'S LEGACY

Corn Tempura
Zucchini-Tomato Gratin
Grilled Thyme Pork Chops

ᴏ

September marks the end of summer, yet it is the ideal time, especially in the Northeast, to enjoy the plenty of the garden. Corn, tomatoes, and zucchini are at their best, and these vegetables are less expensively priced than at any other time of year.

In September we are still—partly, at least—in our summer mood. The nights are mild and we continue to enjoy grilling outside, although we do move on from a lighter fish or poultry to something a little more substantial, like the pork chops featured in this menu.

The recipes that follow use the bounty of our late-summer harvest in ways that announce the arrival of fall. The gratin, for example, is made with zucchini and tomatoes, flavored with Parmesan cheese, olive oil, and sprigs of fresh oregano. It can be assembled up to a day ahead.

The Corn Tempura can be prepared partially in advance or on the spur of the moment and served as an appetizer, first course, or accompaniment to the pork. The batter is a simple concoction of corn, flour, ice water, and a single egg.

continued

I like the pork chops grilled, but they are also good cooked on top of the stove—after being macerated with the seasonings, thyme, and olive oil.

Serve this menu with a good, inexpensive red Bordeaux or a white Graves from Bordeaux.

CORN TEMPURA

TOTAL TIME:
ABOUT 45
MINUTES
It is important that you use a nonstick pan and very hot oil for cooking the corn pancakes; monounsaturated canola oil can withstand the high temperatures without burning, although for best results the pan should be cleaned between each batch of four pancakes.

Notice that when you prepare the batter you add only a little water at first to the flour and egg mixture to create a thick batter that you make very smooth with a whisk before adding the remainder of the water. If all the water were added initially, the flour would form into little lumps and the batter would have to be strained.

^{2}/₃ *cup all-purpose flour*

1 *small or medium egg*

1 *cup ice-cold water*

Salt to taste

2 *ears corn, husked and the kernels cut off the cob (about 2 cups)*

^{1}/₂ *cup canola oil*

1. Mix the flour, egg, and ¹/₄ cup of the water in a bowl with a whisk until very smooth. Add the remaining water and salt and mix again until smooth. Refrigerate until ready to cook. (The batter can be made a few hours ahead.)

2. At cooking time, stir the corn kernels into the batter. Heat 2 tablespoons of the oil in a nonstick 10- or 12-inch skillet. When hot, spoon 3 tablespoons of batter per pancake into the skillet; cook 4 pancakes at a time.

3. Using a splatter-guard, cook the pancakes over high heat for 3 minutes, turn them, and cook for 2 minutes on the other side, until crispy and brown. Wipe out the skillet and repeat with the remaining oil and batter. Or, to make the pancakes faster, use two skillets.

4. As you finish cooking each batch of pancakes, arrange them in one layer on wire racks so air circulates under them. (Although the pancakes are best when made at the last moment, they can be reheated in a hot oven or under the broiler if made ahead.) Serve as an hors d'oeuvre, a first course, or an accompaniment to the pork.

YIELD: 6 SERVINGS (18 3-INCH PANCAKES)

*S*PECIAL TIP: *Add other thinly sliced raw vegetables from your refrigerator to the tempura batter— anything from onions to parsley, carrots, or zucchini. Stir them into the batter and spoon 1 large ladleful (4 ounces) of the mixture at a time into a 9-inch nonstick skillet. Spread the mixture out evenly with a spatula and cook over medium to high heat for about 4 minutes on each side. Serve as a main course for a light lunch, or serve for dinner as a meat or fish garnish.*

ZUCCHINI-TOMATO GRATIN

This colorful gratin can be prepared and assembled, ready for the oven, up to one day ahead. Fresh oregano will add the most flavor, of course, but dried can be used if none is available.

TOTAL TIME: ABOUT 45 MINUTES

4   *zucchini (about 1 1/2 pounds), each about 6 inches long*

3   *large ripe tomatoes (about 1 1/2 pounds)*

1/2   *teaspoon salt*

1/2   *teaspoon freshly ground black pepper*

3   *tablespoons grated Parmesan cheese*

3   *sprigs fresh oregano (about 30 leaves) or 1/2 teaspoon dried oregano*

1/4   *cup olive oil*

continued

1. Trim the zucchini and halve it crosswise. Then cut each half into 4 slices. Cut each tomato crosswise into 12 slices.

2. Arrange alternating slices of the tomato and zucchini in a 15- by 9- by 2-inch gratin dish. Sprinkle the vegetables with the salt, pepper, cheese, oregano, and, finally, the olive oil. (The gratin can be prepared to this point up to a day ahead, covered, and refrigerated until cooking time.)

3. At serving time, place the gratin in a preheated 400-degree oven and cook for 35 minutes, or until the vegetables are tender and moist.

YIELD: 6 SERVINGS

GRILLED THYME PORK CHOPS

TOTAL TIME:
ABOUT 15
MINUTES

You can also cook these chops on top of the stove if need be. Place the seasoned pork chops in a very hot, heavy skillet—cast iron or heavy-weight aluminum is best—and cook for the same time as on the grill.

6 *pork chops, about 8 ounces each and 1 inch thick, as lean as possible (loin chops, although slightly more expensive than rib chops, are the best choice)*

¹/₂ *teaspoon salt*

¹/₂ *teaspoon freshly ground black pepper*

1 *teaspoon dried thyme*

2 *tablespoons olive oil*

1. Trim most of the fat from around the pork chops and sprinkle them with the salt, pepper, and thyme. Pour the oil over the chops.

2. Place the chops on a very hot grill, about 2 to 3 inches from the heat. Cover and cook for about 4 minutes on each side. Set aside in a warm place off the heat for about 5 minutes before serving; they will continue to cook in their own heat, and will be uniformly juicy throughout.

NOTE: If your grill doesn't have a lid, cook the chops a minute longer on each side.

YIELD: 6 SERVINGS

EASING INTO AUTUMN

Cold Zucchini Terrine
Lamb Chops Champvallon
Bread and Banana Pudding

My family loves lamb—roasted, grilled, sautéed, or stewed. Often we roast or grill the leg, which is less expensive than the rack or chops. For braising and for stew, we sometimes use the breast, a very inexpensive, moist, and flavorful cut.

The French usually make a classic dish—côtelettes d'agneau Champvallon—with chops from the rack, but in this variation I use shoulder blade chops from the end of the rack. This cut is meaty and tasty, has few bones, and results in a better dish than one made with traditional chops—which are three times more expensive. It is a hearty dish, a perfect transition to autumn.

Cold Zucchini Terrine, a specialty of Provence, is quite easy and inexpensive to make, especially in early fall, when zucchini is plentiful. Although terrines are usually made with an assortment of vegetables layered according to color, this simple puree, with olive oil, garlic, parsley, and seasonings, is quite pleasant and satisfying.

continued

The raw tomato-basil sauce is delicious, especially when made with fresh, very ripe tomatoes. When regular tomatoes are not as nice or red as they should be, I use plum tomatoes, which are fleshy and less watery.

This meal ends with Bread and Banana Pudding. Bananas seem to accumulate at my house until the skins become speckled with black dots and the flesh softens. The fruit is still flavorful at this stage; here it is combined with slightly stale day-old bread to make a delicious pudding.

A sturdy red wine—a Bordeaux or a Cabernet Sauvignon from the Napa Valley—would go well with this menu.

COLD ZUCCHINI TERRINE

TOTAL TIME:
25 MINUTES
PLUS AT LEAST
4 HOURS
REFRIGERATION

Very ripe tomatoes can be simply cut into chunks and pushed directly through a food mill fitted with a fine screen. If your tomatoes are hard and unripe, puree them first in the bowl of a food processor before straining the mixture through the food mill. If a food mill is not available, push the processed mixture through a sieve or leave it unstrained, if you do not mind eating the seeds and skin of the tomatoes.

FOR THE TERRINE

2 *pounds zucchini*

$^1/_2$ *cup virgin olive oil*

3 TO 4 *cloves garlic, peeled, crushed, and chopped fine*

2 *tablespoons chopped parsley*

1$^1/_2$ *teaspoons salt*

$^1/_2$ *teaspoon freshly ground black pepper*

3 *envelopes unflavored gelatin (about 2$^1/_2$ tablespoons)*

FOR THE TOMATO-BASIL SAUCE

1$^1/_4$ *cups cubed ripe tomatoes (about 2 regular tomatoes or 3 to 4 plum tomatoes)*

1 *tablespoon red wine vinegar*

3 *tablespoons virgin olive oil*

$^1/_4$ *teaspoon Tabasco sauce*

$^1/_2$ *teaspoon salt*

2 TO 3 *tablespoons finely shredded basil*

1. *For the terrine:* Trim the zucchini and cut it into ¼-inch slices. Heat the olive oil in a large saucepan or two skillets and, when hot, add the zucchini in one layer. Sauté over high heat for about 5 minutes, until the zucchini has begun to wilt but still retains its bright color. Stir in the garlic and parsley, cook for about 10 to 15 seconds, and transfer the mixture to the bowl of a food processor. Process for 30 to 40 seconds, until pureed. Transfer the mixture to a bowl and stir in the salt and the pepper.

2. Put 1 cup water in a small saucepan and sprinkle the gelatin on top. When the gelatin has been absorbed, heat the mixture, stirring gently, until the gelatin is melted and the mixture is clear. Add to the pureed zucchini and mix to incorporate. Line a 6-cup loaf pan with plastic wrap and pour the mixture into it. Cover with plastic wrap and refrigerate overnight or for 4 to 5 hours, until well set.

3. *For the tomato-basil sauce:* Push the tomato pieces through a food mill, or puree them first (see above) in a food processor. (The tomato puree can be used unstrained if you don't object to the small pieces of seeds and skin it contains; if you do, strain through a food mill fitted with a fine screen.) You should end up with about 2 cups.

4. Add the vinegar, olive oil, Tabasco, and salt to the tomato puree. Mix well. Stir in the shredded basil and set aside until serving time.

5. To serve, spoon about 3 to 4 tablespoons sauce onto each of six serving plates. Cut the terrine into 1-inch slices and place a slice of the terrine on top of the sauce on each plate. Serve with crunchy bread.

YIELD: 6 SERVINGS

*S*PECIAL TIP: *The raw tomato-basil sauce can be served as a late summer/early autumn soup, and is excellent when tomatoes are at peak flavor. Just add ½ cup water to the puree with a little additional vinegar, olive oil, and salt. Serve with diced cucumbers and croûtons for a refreshing gazpacho.*

LAMB CHOPS CHAMPVALLON

TOTAL TIME:
2 HOURS

The shoulder blade chops are sautéed first and then water is added to the sauté pan. Neither stock nor wine is needed with lamb, which has plenty of taste on its own. The chops are then braised in the oven with sliced potatoes, herbs, onion, and garlic.

The braising liquid should be almost completely absorbed by the time the lamb and potatoes are finished cooking and ready to serve. This dish is as good reheated as fresh.

1   *tablespoon canola or safflower oil*
6   *shoulder-blade lamb chops (about 2 1/2 pounds)*
2   *onions (about 1/2 pound), peeled and sliced (about 2 cups)*
6 TO 7 *cloves garlic, peeled and sliced thin (about 2 tablespoons)*
1 1/2   *teaspoons salt*
3/4   *teaspoon freshly ground black pepper*
2 1/4   *pounds potatoes, peeled, sliced thin, and placed in a bowl with cold water to cover*
1   *bouquet garni, consisting of about 12 sprigs of thyme and 2 to 3 bay leaves tied together into a bunch*
1/4   *cup coarsely chopped parsley*

1. Heat the oil in a large saucepan. When hot, add the lamb chops (3 at a time, if necessary, to avoid crowding) and cook for approximately 4 minutes per side over high heat, until nicely browned. Arrange in one layer in a large gratin dish.

2. Add the sliced onions to the drippings in the pan and sauté, stirring, for about 2 minutes. Add 2 1/2 cups water, the garlic, salt, and pepper.

3. Drain the potato slices well and arrange them on top of the lamb chops. Place the bouquet garni in the middle of the dish and press it gently into the potatoes. Sprinkle the parsley on top and pour the onion mixture and pan juices over the dish.

4. Place the gratin dish on a baking sheet and bake in a 375-degree oven for about 1 1/4 hours, until the potatoes are soft, the lamb is tender, and

142   / FALL

most of the juices have been absorbed. Allow to sit for a few minutes to develop flavor before serving.

YIELD: 6 SERVINGS

BREAD AND BANANA PUDDING

The pudding can be assembled and cooked ahead, but it is best served at room temperature. Serve it alone, or with a dollop of sour cream or a scoop of ice cream.

TOTAL TIME: 35 TO 40 MINUTES

3 *large eggs*

3 *cups milk*

³/₄ *cup honey*

3 *ripe bananas, peeled and cut into ¹/₂-inch slices*

1 *small baguette (about 3 ounces), cut into 15 ¹/₄-inch-thick slices*

2 *tablespoons confectioner's sugar*

1. Beat the eggs gently with a whisk in a bowl, then add the milk and honey and thoroughly mix. Place the banana slices in one layer in the bottom of a 6-cup gratin dish and arrange the bread slices over them, completely covering the bananas. Pour the egg mixture evenly over the bread.

2. Place the gratin dish on a baking sheet and bake in a preheated 375-degree oven for about 25 minutes, until set and slightly puffed. If desired, brown under a hot broiler for a few seconds.

3. Remove from the oven and cool to room temperature. Sprinkle with the confectioner's sugar just before serving.

YIELD: 6 SERVINGS

SEPTEMBER'S RICHES

Corn Salad
Vegetable and Pasta Stew
Grilled Tuna Belly

As it is for many people, September is a time of new beginnings for me, and it puts me in the mood to cook. Happily, fresh fruits and vegetables abound.

Corn is still at its peak, and so this is the time to make Corn Salad, which is delicious served either lukewarm or at room temperature on lettuce leaves. The corn kernels are cut off the cob, and instead of poaching or steaming them, I sauté them for a couple of minutes in the oil that goes into the dressing. Then, while the lightly cooked, slightly crunchy, sweet kernels are still warm, I toss them with the remainder of the seasonings—mustard, vinegar, Tabasco, salt, and sugar.

The Vegetable and Pasta Stew can be made with a wide variety of vegetables. My selection included red onion, scallions, red pepper, zucchini, cauliflower, and eggplant because they were available and reasonably priced at my market when I devised the dish, but you can vary the vegetable assortment at will. Just remember that some vegetables—eggplant, for example—should be cooked longer than others.

continued

Although this stew makes a terrific meal on its own with a green salad, it is paired here with Grilled Tuna Belly. The belly of the tuna was highly prized in cookbooks of old, but now it is often discarded. When I request it, my fishmonger usually gives it to me free of charge; yours may not be as generous, but the cost should still be minimal. Flat, firm, and fatty, the belly is most flavorful, of course, when very fresh. The fattier the fish and the older it is, the stronger the taste.

With this menu, I would suggest fresh fruit for dessert. In early fall, yellow raspberries are in season in the Northeast. If you aren't fortunate enough to find them, choose any of the many other fruits in season, such as peaches or Santa Rosa plums, both of which make a nice dessert.

Try a fruity, slightly spicy white wine from Alsace, in the northeast of France, either a Traminer or a Sylvaner, with this meal. There are very good buys on these wines, and they should be served chilled with this menu.

CORN SALAD

If you want to make this dish ahead, it can be refrigerated, then brought back to room temperature quickly by placing it in a microwave oven for a few seconds, just long enough to take the chill off.

TOTAL TIME:
12 TO 15 MINUTES

6   ears corn, husked (about 3 pounds)

$1/4$ cup canola oil

2   tablespoons red wine vinegar

$1/4$ teaspoon Tabasco sauce

1   tablespoon Dijon-style mustard

1   teaspoon salt

$1/2$ teaspoon sugar

6   leaves lettuce, preferably red-tipped leaf lettuce

1. Using a sharp knife, cut the corn kernels off the cobs. You should have about 5 cups of kernels.

2. Heat the oil in a very large (12-inch) skillet. Add the kernels to the hot oil, and sauté them over high heat for about 3 to 4 minutes, stirring occasionally.

3. Pour the sautéed corn into a bowl and add the vinegar, Tabasco, mustard, salt, and sugar. Mix well. Let cool to lukewarm, or to room temperature.

4. At serving time, arrange a lettuce leaf on each of six plates. Spoon some corn salad into the center of each leaf. Serve immediately.

YIELD: 6 SERVINGS

VEGETABLE AND PASTA STEW

TOTAL TIME:
ABOUT 25
MINUTES

I like to use the same amount of vegetables as pasta in this dish, but you can vary the proportions; if you prefer, cut back on the pasta and add more vegetables, or do the reverse if that is more to your liking. I avoid using a long pasta, such as linguine or noodles, for this stew, selecting instead a compact one—anything from penne to elbow macaroni to bow-tie to gnocchetti, a small pasta that resembles gnocchi, looking like a small closed shell. These types of pasta mix better with vegetables than pastas like spaghetti.

FOR THE VEGETABLES

$^1/_3$ cup virgin olive oil

1 small unpeeled eggplant (about 8 ounces), preferably the small, thin Japanese variety, cut into 1- to $1^1/_2$-inch pieces (about $2^1/_2$ cups)

1 red onion (about 6 ounces), peeled and coarsely chopped (about $1^1/_2$ cups)

10 scallions, dark green and damaged outer leaves removed and discarded, remainder cut into 1-inch pieces (about 1 cup)

1 red bell pepper (about 7 ounces), seeded and cut into $^1/_2$-inch pieces (about $1^1/_2$ cups)

About $^1/_2$ head cauliflower (8 to 10 ounces), divided into flowerets (about 2 cups)

1 zucchini (about 7 ounces), washed, trimmed, and cut into 1-inch pieces (about 2 cups)

$^1/_2$ teaspoon salt

$^1/_2$ teaspoon freshly ground black pepper

FOR THE PASTA

1 pound gnocchetti or other small pasta, like elbow, bow-tie, penne, ziti, or rigate

$^1/_4$ cup grated imported Parmesan cheese, plus additional (optional) for garnish

2 tablespoons virgin olive oil

$^1/_2$ teaspoon salt

$^1/_4$ teaspoon freshly ground black pepper

1. *For the vegetables:* Heat the olive oil in a large skillet. When hot, add the eggplant and cook it over medium to high heat for about 5 minutes, until it is brown on all sides. (It will absorb most of the oil.) Add the red onion, scallions, red pepper, and cauliflower to the skillet. Cover and cook over medium heat for about 5 minutes. Add the zucchini and cook, covered, for another 2 minutes. Add the salt and pepper, toss until well mixed, and set aside.

2. *Meanwhile, for the pasta:* Bring about 4 quarts water to a boil in a large pot. Add the pasta and cook it for 12 to 15 minutes, depending on the size and type of pasta you are using and how you like it cooked.

3. Drain the pasta, reserving ½ cup of the cooking water. Place this water in a large serving bowl, and stir in the ¼ cup cheese, the olive oil, salt, and pepper. Add the pasta and toss it with the cheese mixture.

4. Stir in the reserved vegetables and serve immediately, with extra Parmesan cheese, if desired.

YIELD: 6 SERVINGS

GRILLED TUNA BELLY

I like tuna belly best grilled outside over a very hot fire. If, however, a grill is not available, the belly, seasoned as suggested here, can be cooked under a conventional oven broiler.

TOTAL TIME:
ABOUT 20
MINUTES

2½ *pounds tuna belly (about 2 strips or fillets)*

2 *teaspoons herbes de Provence (see Note)*

1 *teaspoon freshly ground black pepper*

½ *teaspoon salt*

1 *tablespoon olive oil*

FOR THE SAUCE

2 *tablespoons lemon juice*

¼ *cup olive oil*

¼ *teaspoon freshly ground black pepper*

continued

1. With a sharp knife, remove the thick skin from the outer side of the tuna belly and the white filamentlike skin from the other side. Sprinkle both sides with the herbes de Provence, pepper, salt, and olive oil.

2. Place the bellies on the rack of a clean, very hot grill, and cook for 2 minutes. Turn and cook for 1 minute on the other side. Transfer to a 170-degree oven, and let rest in the oven for 10 minutes. (Alternative cooking method: If a grill is not available, cook the fillets under a preheated broiler 3 to 4 inches from the heat for 2 minutes on each side for rare—pink in the center—or longer if you prefer your tuna well done.)

3. *Meanwhile, for the sauce:* Combine all the sauce ingredients in a bowl.

4. Slice the bellies and divide them among six plates. Serve with some sauce spooned on top.

NOTE: If you do not have herbes de Provence, substitute equal amounts of at least three of the following: dried marjoram, thyme, summer savory, sage, fennel, basil, rosemary, and/or lavender.

YIELD: 6 SERVINGS

S PECIAL TIP: *For a tuna salad that is tastier than one made with canned tuna and commercial mayonnaise, flake any leftover grilled tuna belly and mix it with oil, vinegar, salt, freshly ground pepper, mustard, and herbs.*

SPECIALTIES OF
THE SOUTH OF FRANCE

Pissaladière Baguettes
Brandade de Morue au Gratin
Zucchini Salad

There are many mild, beautiful days in October, and these are perfect for gathering some of the vegetables that are still flourishing in the garden or still available at the market. This menu makes use of some of these seasonal vegetables.

Pissaladière, a specialty in the region around Nice, is a type of pizza usually made with fresh bread dough that is covered with onions, anchovy fillets, black olives, and sometimes tomatoes, and baked. This recipe calls for already baked French bread rolls, splitting them and topping the halves with red onion, cherry tomatoes (still juicy and delicious in early fall), garlic, and the *pissalat,* the anchovy and olive oil puree that is the signature of this dish.

Brandade de Morue is a perfect choice for a cool fall evening. Also a specialty of the south of France, this dish is made traditionally with salted codfish, garlic, olive oil, cream, and sometimes potatoes. The recipe that follows calls for more potatoes than are conventionally used, milk instead of cream, less olive oil than is usually called for, and lemon juice and zest for flavor—so it is much less caloric than the original.

Salted codfish from Canada or Portugal is available in small wooden boxes at many specialty food shops and some supermarkets. Ordinarily, it is soaked in cold water overnight, but for this recipe I first wash it and then soak it in cold water for only about two hours before blanching it, draining it, and, finally, cooking it again. This process removes so much salt from the cod that the dish may even need a little additional salt before serving, although I usually do not find it necessary. Rather than serve the brandade on toast, as is traditional, I toast baguette slices and serve them with this earthy dish.

To offset the richness of the pissaladière and brandade, follow them with a light salad of zucchini.

To complete this hearty meal, try a single fresh fruit—perhaps grapes—for dessert. A robust red Spanish wine would complement the meal nicely—for example, some of the good, inexpensive varieties available from Torres.

PISSALADIÈRE BAGUETTES

In Provence, anchovies very often are salted as soon as they are caught, and then pureed later. Here, I crush canned anchovies and their oil with some additional olive oil into a puree, and then brush the cut bread with the resulting *pissalat*. The vegetables and grated Swiss or mozzarella cheese are layered on top and the pissaladière is cooked in the oven. Although this delightful remnant of the summer is a first course here, it also makes a terrific lunch main course with a salad.

TOTAL TIME:
20 MINUTES

3 *French bread rolls (about 2¹/₂ ounces each, 6¹/₂ inches long by 2¹/₂ inches wide) or equivalent-size pieces cut from a baguette*

1 *2-ounce can flat anchovy fillets packed in oil*

3 *tablespoons virgin olive oil*

6 *medium cloves garlic, peeled and sliced very thin*

1 *small red onion (about 4 ounces), peeled and sliced very thin*

24 *cherry tomatoes*

6 *ounces Swiss or mozzarella cheese, grated*

1 *teaspoon dried oregano*

¹/₄ *teaspoon freshly ground black pepper*

¹/₄ *teaspoon salt*

1. Split the rolls in half lengthwise, as for sandwiches. Place the anchovy fillets and their oil in a bowl and chop and crush them with a knife into a puree. Stir in the olive oil to create a *pissalat,* and then brush this mixture on the cut side of each of the split rolls. Cover with the sliced garlic, and then add a layer of sliced onion.

2. Cut the cherry tomatoes in half and arrange 8 halves on each of the 6 roll halves. Sprinkle each with the grated cheese and then sprinkle with the oregano, pepper, and salt.

3. Arrange the rolls on a baking sheet and bake in a preheated 400-degree oven for about 10 minutes, until the cheese is melted and the tomatoes are soft. Serve immediately.

YIELD: 6 SERVINGS

BRANDADE DE MORUE
AU GRATIN

TOTAL TIME:
1 HOUR PLUS
2 HOURS
SOAKING TIME

To make the brandade easier to serve, prepare it ahead and reheat it in a gratin dish at serving time until hot, bubbly, and brown on top. Then either dip the toasts in the brandade or spread some of the mixture on them.

1 *pound salted codfish*

2 *large Idaho potatoes (about 1 pound)*

1 *large lemon*

8 *cloves garlic, peeled*

1¹/₂ *cups hot milk*

¹/₂ *teaspoon freshly ground black pepper*

¹/₈ *teaspoon cayenne pepper*

³/₄ *cup virgin olive oil*

2 *baguettes (about 8 ounces each), cut into 50 ¹/₂-inch-thick rounds*

1. Rinse the cod under cold running water, and place it a large bowl containing about 5 quarts cold water. Let soak for about 2 hours.

2. Meanwhile, wash the potatoes, place them in a saucepan, and cover them with cold water. Bring to a boil, reduce the heat, and boil the potatoes gently for about 45 minutes, until tender. Drain and set aside.

3. Drain the cod and place it in a saucepan with 2 quarts cold water. Bring just to a light boil and drain immediately. Rinse out the pot, and return the cod to the pot with 1 quart cold water. Bring to a boil, reduce the heat, and boil gently for about 10 minutes. Remove from the heat, cover, and let the cod steep in the cooking liquid for about 5 minutes. Drain the cod in a colander and transfer it to a plate, removing and discarding any bones or pieces of skin.

4. Peel the potatoes and cut them into 2-inch pieces. Grate the skin of the lemon (you should have about 1 tablespoon grated lemon rind), and squeeze the lemon to obtain about ¹/₄ cup lemon juice (add some white vinegar, if necessary, to make ¹/₄ cup liquid).

5. Place the cod and the garlic in the bowl of a food processor and process for about 15 seconds, until smooth. Add the lemon rind, potatoes, and hot milk to the cod, and process for about 1 minute, until smooth, stopping to clean the mixture from the sides and push it down into the bottom of the bowl midway through the processing. Add the lemon juice, black pepper, and cayenne pepper, and process briefly to incorporate. Then, with the machine still running, add the oil slowly and continue processing until the mixture is very smooth.

6. Lightly oil an 8-cup gratin dish and transfer the contents of the processor bowl to the dish, spreading it out evenly. Cover with plastic wrap and set aside until ready to serve.

7. At serving time, remove the plastic wrap from the brandade and place it in a 400-degree oven for 10 to 15 minutes, until the top is lightly browned and it is hot throughout. (If the brandade has been refrigerated or is cold, increase the oven cooking time by about 10 minutes to ensure that it is hot.)

8. Meanwhile, make the toasts: Arrange the rounds of bread in a single layer on a cookie sheet. Place in the 400-degree oven for about 10 minutes or until nicely browned.

9. Mound some of the brandade on each of six individual plates. Serve with the toasts for dipping or spreading.

YIELD: 6 TO 7 CUPS

*S*PECIAL TIP: *This recipe makes more than enough brandade for six people. Refrigerate what is left, and use it as a cocktail party hors d'oeuvre, spreading it on small rounds of bread and warming them under the broiler until heated through and nicely browned.*

ZUCCHINI SALAD

TOTAL TIME:
12 MINUTES

For this salad, the zucchini is first cut into thin slices, arranged on a cookie sheet, and placed in a hot oven for a few minutes to draw out some moisture and soften the slices slightly, making them more tender. Then the squash is seasoned simply with salt and pepper, vinegar, and oil.

2 medium-size zucchini (about 1 1/2 pounds total)
1/2 teaspoon salt
1/2 teaspoon freshly ground black pepper
2 tablespoons white wine vinegar
1/4 cup corn or safflower oil

1. Wash the zucchini, trim off and discard the ends, and cut crosswise into 1/4-inch-thick rounds. Arrange the rounds in one layer on a large cookie sheet and sprinkle them with the salt. Place in a preheated 400-degree oven for 5 to 7 minutes, until the rounds render some of their moisture and soften slightly.

2. Transfer the zucchini rounds to a bowl and toss them gently with the pepper, vinegar, and oil. Serve immediately.

YIELD: 6 SERVINGS

AUTUMN'S CATCH

One of the joys of a New England fall is to fish for bluefish. Very often, I drag a net from the shore to pick up the four- to five-inch specimens we call snapper blues. These tiny fish are terrific panfried or sautéed.

When it comes to larger bluefish, however, I take advantage of local seafood markets. Bluefish, available until Thanksgiving, are among the least expensive fish at this time of year and are excellent, providing they are fresh, fresh, fresh!

Bluefish is both extremely nutritious and high in omega-3 fatty acids, which many scientists believe help lower the risk of heart disease. Because it is fatty, large bluefish is ideal for grilling, broiling, or smoking, but it does not fare well prepared in sauces or fried.

The very simple preparation here produces a delicious, fast, and easy dish. Slits are cut through the skin and flesh of the fillets, which are then seasoned and placed under a hot broiler. The heat penetrates the fish through the slits and cooks it in a few minutes, eliminating the need to turn it midway through cooking.

continued

Before cooking, the fish is coated with a mixture of Tabasco, olive oil, and herbs; you can vary the seasonings based on your own preferences. The broiling creates a crisp skin, quite delicious to eat.

For the Puree of Onions, thinly sliced onions are cooked until soft in seasoned water, and the resulting puree is thickened with yellow cornmeal and finished with a few tablespoons of cream.

Cooked Grapes with Cream is a perfect dessert for October, when wine season brings many different kinds of grapes to the market. For this recipe, I use seedless Red Flame grapes, a very firm variety that holds up well to cooking. I cook them in a little water and vinegar for five minutes before seasoning them with lemon juice, lemon rind, honey, and shredded mint. Serve the cooked grapes with a spoonful of sour cream and a cookie or slice of pound cake.

Bluefish, being somewhat assertive in taste, goes well with a chilled red wine, perhaps a Beaujolais or a Gamay, from the Napa Valley.

BROILED PIQUANT BLUEFISH

TOTAL TIME: ABOUT 11 MINUTES

All fish are much better fresh, but this is particularly true of bluefish. Under the blue skin is a layer of dark, fatty flesh, similar to that in tuna; because of this, bluefish tastes mediocre at best after a day, and is even more disappointing if it's been frozen. That is why people often turn up their noses when bluefish is mentioned; previous experience has convinced them that its flavor is too strong. I don't order bluefish in restaurants unless I am confident that I will be served fish that has been caught no more than twenty-four hours before. If you catch your own, be sure to gut them quickly and keep them on ice until cooking time.

3 *medium-size bluefish fillets (14 ounces to 1 pound each, about 1 inch thick)*

1/2 *teaspoon salt*

1 1/2 *teaspoons Italian seasoning*

1 *teaspoon Tabasco sauce*

1 *tablespoon olive oil*

1. Cut each fillet into 2 steaks (7 to 8 ounces each). Cut 2 crosswise slits about 1/4 inch deep through the skin and into the flesh of each fillet. Sprinkle the steaks with the salt, Italian seasoning, Tabasco, and olive oil and arrange them on a broiler pan. Cover and refrigerate until cooking time.

2. When ready to cook, place the pan of fish under a hot broiler, about 3 inches from the source of heat, and broil for 5 to 6 minutes without turning, until the skin begins to blister and brown and the flesh is cooked through. If the fillets are thicker than 1 inch, add 1 to 2 minutes to the cooking time.

3. To serve, slide a fillet, skin side up, onto each plate.

YIELD: 6 SERVINGS

PUREE OF ONIONS

TOTAL TIME:
55 MINUTES

This creamy, flavorful stew goes well not only with fish but with sautéed chicken or roast veal. Although the cooked onions could be pushed through a food mill or processed briefly in a food processor, these machines tend to liquify them too much; it is preferable merely to whip them with a whisk or a spoon to break the slices of onion into a coarse puree.

2 *pounds onions, peeled and sliced thin (approximately 7 cups)*
1 *teaspoon herbes de Provence (see Note, page 150)*
2 *tablespoons peanut oil*
1 1/2 *teaspoons salt*
1/2 *teaspoon freshly ground black pepper*
1/4 *cup yellow cornmeal*
1/4 *cup heavy cream*

1. Place the sliced onions, herbes de Provence, oil, salt, pepper, and 1 cup water in a stainless steel saucepan, bring to boil over high heat, and stir well. Reduce the heat to low, cover, and cook gently for 30 to 35 minutes.

2. Sprinkle the cornmeal on top of the onion mixture, stirring it in as you add it. Cover the pan and continue cooking for 15 minutes, stirring occasionally to prevent scorching.

3. Using a whisk or spoon, stir the mixture vigorously for 1 to 2 minutes to break the onions into smaller pieces and create a puree. Add the cream, stir, bring to boil, and immediately remove from the heat. Serve.

YIELD: 6 SERVINGS

SPECIAL TIP: *Be sure to use a very sharp knife for peeling and slicing the onions for the puree. The more you crush onions as you work with them, the more their sulfurous compounds are released, irritating your eyes and discoloring the onions. If the onions are very strong, place the slices in a sieve and rinse them under cold running water, which will remove some of the irritant and make a milder dish.*

COOKED GRAPES WITH CREAM

TOTAL TIME:
13 MINUTES

Requiring only a few minutes to prepare, this dish is a great use for grapes that have begun to discolor and shrivel and might otherwise be thrown out.

After five minutes of cooking, the skins of the Red Flame grapes will have lost most of their red color, but will just be beginning to blister and break. Softer grape varieties, on the other hand, turn into mush after barely a minute of cooking.

1½ *pounds seedless Red Flame grapes, removed from the stems (about 4 cups)*

1 *tablespoon red wine vinegar*

2 *teaspoons grated lemon rind*

1½ *tablespoons lemon juice*

1 *tablespoon honey*

1 *tablespoon shredded mint leaves*

1 *tablespoon Cognac or other brandy (optional)*

½ *cup sour cream, for garnish*

1. Place the grapes, vinegar, and ½ cup water in a stainless steel saucepan, and bring to a boil over high heat. Reduce the heat to low, cover, and cook gently for about 5 minutes. The skins of the grapes will lose their red color and begin to crack open.

2. Meanwhile, combine the lemon rind, lemon juice, honey, and mint leaves in a bowl. When the grapes are cooked, add them to the mixture in the bowl, stir well, and let cool.

3. Add the Cognac, if desired, and serve in wine glasses, garnished with a spoonful of the sour cream.

YIELD: 6 SERVINGS

⊘

Fromage Fort
Fish and Pasta with Wine Sauce
Sautéed Napa Cabbage

Fromage fort is a special recipe rooted in my childhood. If you, like me, always have little leftover pieces of cheese in your refrigerator, this is the perfect use for it.

As the name indicates, *fromage fort* means strong cheese. It is an assertive, highly seasoned mixture of cheeses and, in the part of France where I come from, near Lyon, everyone has a recipe for it. My father used to make it regularly; mine, patterned after his, is flavored with garlic and white wine. Instead of, or in addition to, white wine, a little leek broth or liquid from a vegetable soup can be used to moisten the cheese.

I often use at least six or seven different types of cheese, although it can be made with a minimum of three, including both hard and soft varieties. Leftover pieces kept too long in the refrigerator may have dried out on the surface and be a bit moldy. Trim off any crust or mold before starting.

Fromage Fort makes a pleasant first course with Fish and Pasta with Wine Sauce.

continued

Fresh fish is becoming more readily available throughout the nation and most supermarkets offer a fairly good selection. Yet fish stores—especially large ones with a big turnover—are usually the best places to buy fresh fish. "Fresh" is the essential word when buying fish—and by fresh I mean fish that has been out of the water no more than twenty-four hours.

Although fish cooks quickly and is versatile, it is, unfortunately, often expensive. Comparison shopping helps, however. You will usually find that fish is not only fresher but also less expensive at an establishment that receives whole fish and cuts them into fillets on the premises.

Buy whole fish and have the fishmonger fillet them for you if you are not proficient at doing it yourself. Freeze the bones for use later in soup or stock.

Be aware that some bottom fish, like grouper, and flat fish, like sole, have large bones and thus yield a low percentage of meat in relation to their weight—ratios are often as low as four ounces of meat per pound of fish. This is in contrast to rounder, bigger fish like salmon, which yield half their weight in meat. Tuna and shark are practically all meat, as are squid and octopus.

Cooked at the last moment, the penne is drained, returned to its cooking pot, and mixed with some of the wine sauce. This helps keep the pasta from sticking together and enables you to stir and season it before serving. The fish and the remainder of the sauce is spooned over the pasta on a serving platter or individual plates. The dish can be served with grated Parmesan cheese.

In the vegetable dish here, Napa cabbage is sautéed (while the pasta is cooking) in a little vegetable oil and a dash of butter and seasoned with salt and pepper. It makes a refreshing accompaniment to meat as well as fish dishes.

A simple Beaujolais would be a good wine to serve with this menu.

FROMAGE FORT

Fromage fort is best eaten on bread or toast. As a child, I especially loved it toasted. I would spread the cheese mixture on a thick slab of country bread, impale the bread on a fork, and then hold it in the fireplace, with the cheese side as close as possible to the fire. When the cheese bubbled and a nice glaze formed, I would rub the crusty cheese with a piece of butter and eat it piping hot. Although I have a strong emotional attachment to the preparations surrounding that early taste memory, I find that the bread glazes just as well when placed under the broiler for a few minutes. Refrigerated, this original and economical cheese combination will keep for a week or two.

TOTAL TIME:
10 TO 15 MINUTES

3 TO 4 *garlic cloves, peeled*

1 *pound leftover cheese, a combination of as many hard and soft varieties as you like (such as Brie, Cheddar, Swiss, bleu, mozzarella, or goat), pieces trimmed to remove surface dryness and mold*

1/2 *cup dry white wine, leek broth, vegetable broth, or a mixture of these*

1 *teaspoon freshly ground black pepper*

Salt, if needed (see Note)

1. Place the peeled garlic in the bowl of a food processor and process for a few seconds, until coarsely chopped. Add the cheese, white wine and/or broth, pepper, and salt, if needed, and process for 30 to 45 seconds, until the mixture is soft and creamy but not too smooth. Place in a crock, cover with plastic wrap, and refrigerate until ready to use.

2. To serve, spread generously on bread or toast and eat cold; or arrange on a tray and place under a hot broiler for a few minutes to melt the cheese before serving.

NOTE: If you use only unsalted cheeses or a large amount of unsalted farmer's cheese, for example, you may want to add a little salt. Usually, however, cheese is salty enough so that additional salt is not needed.

YIELD: MAKES 2 CUPS, ENOUGH FOR ABOUT 50 TOASTS

FISH AND PASTA WITH
WINE SAUCE

TOTAL TIME:
30 TO 40
MINUTES

The Fish and Pasta with Wine Sauce recipe is made with scrod, whose white tender meat is usually relatively inexpensive. Depending on market availability, other inexpensive choices for this recipe are whiting, which should be cut into crosswise pieces (leaving the center bone), or fillets of blowfish (sea squab or puffer), haddock, cod, or shark.

To have everything ready to serve at the same time, assemble all the ingredients first, put the pasta water on to heat, and then start the sauce. I use penne, a tube-like pasta cut on an angle into one-and-a-half-inch lengths. Penne is also one of my favorite pastas to cook with beans, as it holds its shape and absorbs the flavor of other ingredients well.

1 *large lemon*

$^1/_2$ *cup virgin olive oil*

2 *cups coarsely chopped onions (about 2 to 3 onions, depending on the size)*

2 *teaspoons dried thyme*

6 TO 8 *garlic cloves, peeled and coarsely chopped (about 2 tablespoons)*

1 *8-ounce bottle clam juice*

$1^1/_2$ *teaspoons salt*

$1^1/_2$ *teaspoons freshly ground black pepper*

$1^1/_2$ *pounds penne or other pasta such as elbows or shells*

$1^1/_2$ *pounds scrod fillets, completely cleaned and cut into 2-inch pieces about $^3/_4$ inch thick*

6 *tablespoons chopped parsley or shredded basil, for garnish*
Grated Parmesan cheese (optional)

1. Bring about 4 quarts water to a boil in a large pot set over high heat. Meanwhile, with a vegetable peeler, remove 10 to 12 strips from the outermost surface of the skin of the lemon, which contains the essential oils and thus is the most flavorful part of the skin. Stack them up together and cut them into very thin julienne strips. This should yield approximately 3 tablespoons.

2. Heat the oil in a medium saucepan. When hot, add the onions and thyme and cook over medium heat for about 3 minutes. Add the garlic, julienned lemon peel, clam juice, $3/4$ cup water, and 1 teaspoon each of the salt and pepper. Bring to a boil and boil about 1 minute.

3. As soon as the water in the large pot comes to a boil, add the pasta with a dash of salt and stir. Bring the water back to the boil and boil for about 10 to 12 minutes, depending on whether you like your pasta al dente or more tender.

4. While the pasta is cooking, add the pieces of fish to the sauce and bring the sauce just back to the boil. Remove from the heat, cover, and set aside until serving time.

5. As soon as the pasta is cooked, drain it in a colander and return it to the pot in which it was cooked. Pour about $1/2$ cup of the wine sauce over the pasta and toss to moisten the pasta. Add the remaining $1/2$ teaspoon each of salt and pepper and toss again.

6. Arrange the pasta either on a large platter or on individual plates and top with the reminder of the sauce and the pieces of fish. Garnish with the parsley or basil and serve immediately, with Parmesan cheese if desired.

YIELD: 6 SERVINGS

SAUTÉED NAPA CABBAGE

TOTAL TIME:
10 MINUTES
Napa cabbage, a tight, white, tender oblong variety of cabbage, is also excellent in salad or soup, or stir-fried Chinese style.

1 *large or 2 small heads Napa cabbage (about 2 pounds), cut into 1 1/2-inch chunks (about 14 to 15 cups, lightly packed)*
3 *tablespoons safflower or canola oil*
2 *tablespoons unsalted butter*
1/2 *teaspoon freshly ground black pepper*
1/2 *teaspoon salt*

1. Wash the cabbage in a sink filled with cold water, lifting it in and out of the water, and drain it in a colander.

2. Heat the oil in a saucepan until hot, add the butter, and, as soon as it melts, add the still-wet cabbage. Cover and cook over medium to high heat, stirring occasionally, for 4 to 5 minutes, until the cabbage is wilted and tender but still slightly firm. The cabbage will sizzle initially but then will stew as the moisture emerges from it. Stir in the pepper and salt, and serve immediately.

YIELD: 6 SERVINGS

TWO MEALS FROM
ONE SAVORY PORK ROAST

Cabbage and Basil Salad
Corn off the Cob
Braised Pork Roast with Sweet Potatoes

Pork and Potato Hash

My wife, Gloria, loves pork dishes, especially those with beans and rice or with plantain bananas or sweet potatoes. As a result, pork, in one form or another, is featured often at our house when cool weather sets in. It is one of the best values on the market, a versatile meat that is good served in stews as well as roasted or grilled, and it is indispensable when ground for sausage, pâtés, and meat dumplings.

The pork roast lends itself to slow, long-simmering casserole cooking and so is often garnished with dried beans, lentils, or other legumes that require a long time to cook. The juice of the roast greatly flavors whatever is cooked with it, from beans to garlic, onions, and potatoes.

I first cook the pork slowly for one hour with water and seasonings to moisturize it. Then I add the other ingredients and place the casserole in the oven, uncovered, to braise the meat and reduce the liquid to a concentrated juice.

This braising technique, whereby some of the liquid is used to moisturize the meat, produces a tender, succulent roast and delicious garnishes.

continued

The roast is flavored with a little honey, cumin, and soy sauce to produce a wonderful natural gravy, and the sweet potatoes cooked with it become very soft and creamy.

The menu begins with the Cabbage and Basil Salad and the Corn off the Cob, followed by the braised Pork Roast with Sweet Potatoes, although the corn can be served with the pork.

Fresh corn is still available in mid-autumn. Each ear yields about one cup of kernels, which are cooked for a few minutes to produce a crunchy but tender side dish.

The Cabbage and Basil Salad is best made with pale green cabbage, which is sweet. The cabbage is shredded as for a conventional coleslaw and the dressing is made of garlic, mustard, vinegar, and olive oil, with the shredded basil added at the end.

A light dessert of fresh or poached fruit would provide a good finish to this robust fall dinner, and a deep red, earthy, country-style wine would complement the meal nicely.

With the leftover pork the next day, I make an earthy Pork and Potato Hash. For this dish, sliced potatoes are first combined with diced onions in a skillet and boiled for 10 minutes, until tender. Then the leftover pork is added with the rest of the seasonings and the hash is cooked until all the moisture evaporates and the mixture browns on the bottom.

It is essential to use a nonstick pan. When first boiled, the potatoes release starch, which makes the mixture very sticky. Eventually, the mixture begins to form a crust in the bottom of the pan. This crust should be stirred into the mixture every few minutes, especially during the last 10 minutes of cooking, to produce a hash that is moist and soft with a lot of crusty pieces in it. At the end, a thick crust forms on the bottom and the hash does not stick anymore.

The hash, with or without fried eggs, can be served with a salad for a new menu.

CABBAGE AND BASIL SALAD

TOTAL TIME: 10 MINUTES

This salad can be made a few hours ahead so the cabbage has time to soften and develop more taste, and it should be eaten at room temperature. The cabbage in any leftover salad will eventually be "cooked" a little by the vinegar and soften somewhat, but it will still be crunchy and flavorful enough to taste good on sandwiches the next day.

1 *small head green cabbage (about 1 1/4 pounds)*

FOR THE DRESSING

4 *cloves garlic, peeled, crushed, and chopped fine (about 1 tablespoon)*

3/4 *teaspoon salt*

1/2 *teaspoon freshly ground black pepper*

1 *tablespoon mustard, preferably Dijon-style*

2 *tablespoons red wine vinegar*

1/4 *cup virgin olive oil*

1/4 *cup shredded basil*

1. Cut the cabbage in half and remove the center rib. Shred as you would for coleslaw. You should have about 6 to 7 cups of lightly packed cabbage.

2. *For the dressing:* Combine the garlic, salt, pepper, mustard, vinegar, and olive oil in a bowl, stirring the ingredients with a whisk. Add the cabbage and stir.

3. Just before serving, sprinkle the basil on top.

YIELD: 6 SERVINGS

PECIAL TIP: *The dressing for this salad will keep, refrigerated, for up to a week. Double the ingredients, place them in a jar with a tight-fitting lid, and shake well. Use the excess dressing to season salads, poached vegetables, or fish.*

CORN OFF THE COB

TOTAL TIME:
15 MINUTES

Cooked this way, the kernels remain crunchy and sweet. Because the sugar in corn begins to turn to starch as soon as it is picked, the corn will be sweeter if used immediately.

6 *ears corn*

1 *tablespoon canola oil*

2 *tablespoons unsalted butter*

$^1/_2$ *teaspoon salt*

1. Remove the husks from the corn and cut the kernels off the cobs with a sharp knife. You should have about 5 to 6 cups of kernels.

2. Place the kernels in a saucepan with $^1/_2$ cup water and the oil, butter, and salt. Bring to a boil over high heat, stirring. Cover and continue to boil over high heat for about 2 to 3 minutes. Serve immediately.

YIELD: 6 SERVINGS

BRAISED PORK ROAST WITH SWEET POTATOES

This braised pork roast dish blends three cultural influences. Highly seasoned in the Puerto Rican manner, it demonstrates classical French cooking techniques and captures a traditional American taste I have learned to love.

TOTAL TIME: 2 HOURS AND 10 MINUTES

If possible, select a roast from the pork shoulder butt (or, if unavailable, the sirloin tip), which is inexpensive, tender, and more moist than the center cut.

1 *3-pound shoulder butt pork roast (boneless)*

2 *tablespoons dark soy sauce*

¹/₂ *teaspoon Tabasco sauce*

2 *tablespoons red wine vinegar or cider vinegar*

2 *tablespoons honey*

1 *teaspoon cumin*

2 *pounds sweet potatoes (about 4)*

1 *pound onions (about 2 large)*

6 *large cloves garlic, peeled*

1. Place the pork roast in a cast-iron or enamel casserole with a lid. Add 2 cups water and the soy sauce, Tabasco, vinegar, honey, and cumin. Bring to a boil, reduce the heat to very low, and boil gently, covered, for 1 hour.

2. Meanwhile, peel the sweet potatoes and cut into 1¹/₂-inch slices. Peel the onions and cut each into 4 to 6 wedges, depending on their size.

3. After the pork has cooked for 1 hour, add the sweet potatoes, onions, and garlic. Bring back to the boil and boil gently, covered, for about 15 minutes.

4. Uncover the casserole and place it in the center of a preheated 375-degree oven. Cook for 45 minutes, turning the meat in the juices every 15 minutes. At the end of the cooking period, the juices should be dark and concentrated, the meat tender when pierced with a fork, and the vegetables very soft.

5. Serve directly from the casserole, cutting the meat at the table.

YIELD: 6 SERVINGS

PORK AND POTATO HASH

Good (made it with turkey dark meat)

TOTAL TIME: 50 MINUTES

This recipe contains about two and a half cups of leftover pork. If you have less, substitute other meat—ham or chicken, for example—or add more potatoes. Although hash is traditionally served with a fried egg on top, I've listed this only as an optional garnish.

- 1¾ *pounds all-purpose potatoes, peeled, cut into ¼-inch slices, and rinsed in cold water*
- 2 *medium-size onions (about ¾ pound), peeled and cut into ½-inch dice*
- *A few tablespoons of juice leftover from the Braised Pork Roast (page 173), if any remains*
- 3 TO 4 *cloves garlic, peeled, crushed, and chopped (about 1 tablespoon)*
- ⅓ *cup minced scallions (3 to 4 scallions)*
- 3 *tablespoons olive oil*
- ¼ *teaspoon Tabasco sauce*
- ¾ *teaspoon salt*
- 2 *teaspoons Worcestershire sauce*
- 10 TO 12 *ounces leftover pork roast, from Braised Pork Roast, cut into ½-inch dice (about 2½ cups)*
- 1 *fried egg, for garnish (optional)*

1. Place the sliced potatoes, 1½ cups water, the onions, and the juice from the pork roast in a 12-inch nonstick skillet (or two smaller nonstick skillets). Bring to a boil, cover, and boil over medium heat for 10 minutes. Then add the garlic, scallions, olive oil, Tabasco, salt, Worcestershire sauce, and pork. Mix well and cook, uncovered, over high heat, stirring, for about 5 minutes.

2. Most of the moisture will have evaporated by now and the mixture should be starting to sizzle. Since the hash will begin to stick at this point, use a flat wooden spatula to scrape up the crusty bits sticking to the bottom of the pan and stir them into the uncooked mixture. Continue to cook over medium heat for about 20 minutes, stirring every 3 to 4 minutes at first. The mixture will brown faster in the last 10 minutes of cooking and should be stirred every 2 to 3 minutes.

3. At the end of the cooking time, the moisture will have evaporated and the mixture will no longer be sticking to the pan. Press down on the mixture to make it hold together and fold the solid mass into an oval omelet shape. Invert onto a large platter. Serve immediately as is or with the fried egg on top.

YIELD: 6 SERVINGS

COLD WEATHER WARM-UP

Fiery Chili with Red Beans
Boiled Rice
Apple Fritters

One-dish meals are very popular in my house, and when the cold weather comes, I long for chili. Many years ago a friend sent me a recipe that had been given to her by the warden of San Quentin Prison. It was hot, very hot, but we all loved it. Even though I lost the recipe long ago, the taste of that chili remains in my memory, and I think the recipe here is close to the real McCoy.

I always serve chili with boiled long-grain white rice, garnish it with shredded sharp Cheddar cheese and chopped red or white onion, and accompany it with hot corn tortillas or dry tacos. Even though I know that "real" Texas chili doesn't include beans, we make ours with red kidney beans or another variety of dried beans. We like it better that way, and the beans extend the dish greatly, make it more healthful, more of a complete meal, and more economical, because the quantity of meat added can be reduced.

The spice mixture for the chili includes dry mustard, cumin powder, red pepper flakes, chili powder, and coriander seeds. I grind the seeds to a powder in a mini-chop or small coffee grinder. If you don't have one of these small devices, use a mortar and pestle or the bottom of a heavy saucepan to crush the seeds.

Apple Fritters make a delightful dessert to serve after chili. They are made with a simple batter consisting of a cup of flour, a cup of ice-cold water, and one egg.

With this hot meal, I suggest a simple green salad, and beer or jug wine, perhaps a hearty Gallo Burgundy or an Almadèn Chablis.

FIERY CHILI WITH RED BEANS

TOTAL TIME:
2 HOURS AND
45 MINUTES

Although any type of beef can be used in this recipe, the best choice is chuck, shoulder, or shank, all of which are moist and tender. I like the meat coarsely chopped, in $1/4$-inch pieces, not finely chopped or ground.

2 *pounds dried red kidney beans*

1 *tablespoon salt*

2 *pounds stewing beef (chuck), cut into 1-inch pieces*

$1/2$ *pound rind pieces from a ham, or bacon, cut into $1/2$-inch pieces*

1 *pound onions, peeled and cut into 1-inch dice*

8 *cloves garlic, peeled, crushed, and chopped (about 2 tablespoons)*

2 *tablespoons chopped jalapeño pepper (or more or less, to taste)*

1 *28-ounce can whole Italian tomatoes in juice*

2 *teaspoons coriander seeds*

2 *teaspoons cumin powder*

2 *teaspoons dry mustard*

1 *teaspoon red pepper flakes*

$1/4$ *cup chili powder*

1 *cup grated Cheddar cheese, for garnish*

1 *cup chopped onion, washed in a sieve and pressed dry in a kitchen towel to prevent discoloration, for garnish*

Tabasco sauce, for garnish

Corn tortillas or tacos

1. Rinse the beans under cool water, removing and discarding any damaged ones or any foreign material. Place the beans in a large pot with 12 cups cold water and 1 teaspoon of the salt, and bring to a boil. Cover, reduce the heat, and cook gently for 1 1/4 to 1 1/2 hours, until tender but not mushy. Set the beans aside in their own liquid.

2. Chop the beef pieces coarsely by hand or in a food processor (place about 1/2 pound of the chuck at a time in the bowl of a food processor and pulse the motor for about 10 seconds, until the beef is coarsely chopped).

3. Place the pieces of ham rind or bacon in a saucepan and cook over medium heat for about 10 minutes, until most of the fat has been rendered and the rind is dry and brown. Add the diced onions and the beef and cook, stirring, for about 5 minutes, until the meat breaks up and loses its red color. Stir in the garlic, jalapeño pepper, and tomatoes.

4. Using a mini-chop or small coffee grinder, process the coriander seeds to a paste. Add with the cumin powder, mustard, red pepper flakes, chili powder, and the remaining 2 teaspoons salt to the saucepan. Bring the mixture to a boil. Add to the beans (and their liquid), bring to the boil, cover, reduce the heat to low, and simmer for 1 hour. (The mixture will be soupy).

5. Spoon over the boiled rice, and garnish with the Cheddar cheese, chopped onion, and Tabasco sauce. Pass the corn tortillas or tacos to eat with the chili.

YIELD: 12 SERVINGS

S PECIAL TIP: *Chili con carne is, of course, an ideal dish to make ahead. It freezes well and will keep under refrigeration for four days to one week. It actually improves in flavor with reheating. Freeze the chili in small enough containers so that you can thaw it easily on short notice.*

BOILED RICE

TOTAL TIME:
25 MINUTES

1   *tablespoon corn oil*
2   *cups white long-grain rice*
1   *teaspoon salt*

1.   Place the oil and rice in a saucepan and mix well. Add 4 cups water and the salt, and bring to a boil, stirring occasionally, over high heat. Cover tightly, reduce the heat to very low, and simmer gently for 20 minutes.

2.   Fluff with a fork and serve with the chili.

YIELD: 12 SERVINGS

APPLE FRITTERS

TOTAL TIME:
12 MINUTES

Use the least expensive apples you can find, as any variety works well in this recipe. Notice that the apples are not peeled; they are stood upright and cut on all sides into half-inch-thick slices as far as the core, which is then discarded. The apple slices are stacked and cut into sticks, and these sticks are mixed into the batter. Large spoonfuls of the mixture cook in just a few minutes in hot oil.

If you make the fritters ahead, be sure to cook them until they are crisp and well browned. Then reheat and recrisp them in a toaster oven or under the broiler just before serving them heavily dusted with granulated sugar.

1   *cup all-purpose flour*
1   *large egg*
1   *cup ice-cold water*
1   *pound apples (about 3), any variety*
1 1/2   *cups canola oil*
1/2   *cup granulated sugar, for dusting the fritters*

1.   Place the flour, egg, and one third of the water in a bowl and mix vigorously with a whisk. The mixture will be fairly thick. When smooth, add the remaining water, and mix again until the water is incorporated and the batter is thin and smooth.

2.   Stand the unpeeled apples upright on a board, and cut each one vertically into $1/2$-inch slices, stopping when you reach the core, pivoting the apple, and cutting again, until only the core remains. Discard the cores, stack the apple slices, and cut them into $1/2$-inch sticks (you should have 4 cups). Stir the apple sticks into the batter.

3.   Heat the oil to 375 degrees in a large heavy skillet. When hot, pour about $1/3$ cup of the batter into the pan for each fritter, making about 4 or 5 at a time. Using two forks, spread the batter out so each fritter is no more than $1/2$ inch thick. Cook for about 3 minutes on each side, until brown and crisp.

4.   Drain the fritters on paper towels and transfer them to a rack. Sprinkle liberally with the sugar, and serve immediately.

YIELD: ABOUT 12 FRITTERS

Special tip   VEGETABLE FRITTERS: *Instead of adding apples to the fritter batter, stir in some thinly sliced leftover vegetables—anything from carrots to parsley, onions, and zucchini. Drop large spoonfuls of the mixture into a very hot, heavy skillet that has been generously oiled with corn or canola oil, and cook them for approximately 3 to 4 minutes on each side. Serve 1 large pancake per person as a vegetable side dish with a roast or stew.*

Turkey and Cranberries: A New Look

Turkey Cutlets in Anchovy-Lemon Sauce
Gratin of Butternut Squash
Cranberry Kisel

೮

Like most Americans, I feel that it is not Thanksgiving without a large roast turkey, and I usually serve one on Christmas as well. I love turkey and prepare it in various ways throughout the year, sometimes stewing the legs and serving them with rice, sometimes grilling the wings on a barbecue, and often cooking the breast, as I do here, in the style of veal. If properly cooked, turkey breasts make very moist, tender cutlets. Turkey breasts are lean, low in cholesterol, and readily available in most supermarkets.

The turkey cutlets in this menu are accented with a sauce made of pureed anchovies and lemon juice. It enhances the somewhat bland flavor of the meat, giving it more character.

In the spirit of the season, I serve the cutlets in the fall with a Gratin of Butternut Squash. Squash is inexpensive then, and of the many varieties available at the market, butternut is one of the creamiest and richest. It is excellent halved, seeded, scored, and roasted in the oven with a little butter and honey.

continued

For this recipe, the squash is peeled, removing the surface skin and underlying green layer, then sliced and cooked briefly in water. I toss it with a little olive oil and butter, and sprinkle it with salt, pepper, and Parmesan cheese. Serve it hot, reheating under the broiler or in the oven if it has been prepared in advance.

Cranberries, plentiful at holiday time, are usually made into a relish or sauce. Although a slightly altered version of my cranberry recipe can be served as a sauce with roast turkey (see Special Tip, page 187), I serve it as a dessert here with sour cream.

A Moselle or Alsatian Riesling wine would be my choice for this menu.

TURKEY CUTLETS
IN ANCHOVY-LEMON SAUCE

TOTAL TIME:
35 MINUTES
(OR 10 MINUTES
IF USING
BONELESS
TURKEY
BREAST)

Pound for pound, unboned turkey breast is about half the cost of ready-to-sauté turkey steaks. Although this cost advantage disappears when your butcher bones the breast, you still have the bonus of the wings, bones, and skin for use in other dishes. Reserve the bones for soup or stew, and either discard the skin, or spread it out on a cookie sheet and roast it in a 400-degree oven for 20 to 30 minutes, until brown and crisp, for use as crackling to garnish soups and salads.

1 *whole (double) turkey breast (see Note)*
1 *2-ounce can flat anchovy fillets*
2 *tablespoons lemon juice*
1¹/₂ *tablespoons unsalted butter*
1 *teaspoon salt*
¹/₂ *teaspoon freshly ground black pepper*
2 *tablespoons chopped parsley, for garnish*

1. To bone the turkey breast, first remove the wings at the joints; reserve them to use in another recipe. Pull off the skin and discard it or prepare it as crackling (see above). Cut around the breastbone and remove the meat from each side in one large piece. Holding the knife at an angle, cut each piece lengthwise into 3 large steaks, and pound them lightly to make them equal in size. Set aside until cooking time.

2. Drain the anchovies, reserving the oil. You should have approximately 2 tablespoons oil. Chop the anchovies coarsely and put them in a bowl. Toss with the lemon juice, and set aside.

3. Heat the butter and anchovy oil in one large or two smaller skillets. Sprinkle the cutlets with the salt and pepper. When the butter and oil are hot, add the cutlets and sauté them for about 1 1/2 minutes on each side. They should still be pink inside.

4. Transfer the cutlets to an ovenproof baking pan. Add the anchovy-lemon juice mixture to the juices in the skillet(s), mix well, and pour over the cutlets. Place in a preheated 200-degree oven for 15 to 20 minutes. At that point, if not serving immediately, reduce the heat to 170 to 180 degrees; serve within 30 to 40 minutes. Garnish the cutlets with the chopped parsley.

NOTE: A whole breast will yield 1/2 pound skin, 2 1/4 to 2 1/2 pounds bones (including wings), and 2 to 2 1/2 pounds meat. If you prefer, you can substitute 6 boneless turkey steaks or 2 to 2 1/2 pounds other boneless turkey meat for the turkey breast.

YIELD: 6 SERVINGS

GRATIN OF BUTTERNUT SQUASH

TOTAL TIME:
30 MINUTES

This is a great do-ahead dish. The squash can be peeled, blanched, and combined with the other ingredients early in the day and then reheated briefly at serving time.

1   *butternut squash (about 3 pounds)*
2   *tablespoons olive oil*
1   *tablespoon unsalted butter, softened*
³/₄ *teaspoon salt*
¹/₂ *teaspoon freshly ground black pepper*
2   *tablespoons grated Parmesan cheese*

1. With a small sharp knife or vegetable peeler, carefully peel the squash, removing both the yellow skin and the green layer underneath. (The skin is difficult to remove, and you will have to peel the squash twice if you are using a vegetable peeler.) Cut the squash in half lengthwise and remove the seeds. Cut in half lengthwise again, then cut crosswise into ¹/₂-inch slices.

2. Place the squash slices in a large saucepan and cover with tepid tap water. Bring to a boil over high heat, reduce the heat, and boil gently for 3 to 4 minutes, until tender. Drain in a colander and transfer to a gratin dish. Mix in the olive oil, butter, salt, and pepper. Sprinkle with the cheese.

3. If serving the gratin immediately, run it under a hot broiler for a few minutes to brown it lightly on top. If the squash has been prepared in advance, reheat it in a 425-degree oven for 15 minutes, until hot throughout and lightly browned on top. Serve immediately.

YIELD: 6 SERVINGS

CRANBERRY KISEL

This his recipe is inspired by the traditional Russian *kisel*, consisting of a sweetened puree of fruit—conventionally loganberries and cranberries—lightly thickened and served in glass goblets.

TOTAL TIME: 20 MINUTES

1 *12-ounce package fresh cranberries*

1 *tablespoon grated orange rind*

1 *cup orange juice*

$^1/_3$ *cup sugar*

1 *teaspoon cornstarch*

$^1/_2$ *cup sour cream or sweetened whipped cream, for garnish (optional)*

1. Put all the ingredients but the sour cream in a stainless steel saucepan and bring to a boil over high heat, stirring occasionally. Reduce the heat, cover, and cook gently for approximately 10 minutes. The mixture will be thick and bright red. Set aside to cool.

2. When cool, divide among six glass goblets. Garnish, if desired, with the sour cream or sweetened whipped cream, and serve with cookies, if you like.

YIELD: 2 CUPS

*S*PECIAL TIP   CRANBERRY RELISH: *To transform the dessert into a spicy cranberry relish, add $^1/_4$ teaspoon cayenne pepper, $^1/_4$ teaspoon nutmeg, and $^1/_8$ teaspoon ground cloves to the saucepan in the first step. Then proceed according to the recipe, omitting the sour cream garnish. Refrigerated in a tightly covered jar, the relish will keep for a few weeks. Serve cold with roast turkey, goose, or other poultry, or with roast pork.*

Winter

GOOD FOR THE SOUL: TWO MENUS WITH A SOUTHERN ACCENT

MENU 1.

Seafood Gumbo
Chicken Livers in Salad
Bread and Raisin Pudding

MENU 2.

Celery and Apple Salad
Black-eyed Peas and Kale Ragout
Hot Wine
Cozy Cider

COMFORTING FOOD FOR A COLD WINTER DAY

Pumpkin and Pastina Soup
Squid à l'Ail
Carrot and Sunflower Seed Salad

HEARTY FARE IN AN ORIENTAL MOOD

Bread and Onion Pancakes
Sautéed Soy Chicken
Baked Yams

FOR THE ADVENTUROUS GOURMET

Chicken Hearts and Gizzards Soup
Catfish with Croûtons and Nuts
Pears in Mint and Tea

DO-AHEAD DISHES FOR BUSY DAYS

Cauliflower Soup
Lamb and Yams Fricassee
Apple Stew

BUDGET-MINDED COMPANY FARE

Grilled Eggplant Oriental
Veal Tendrons and Tarragon Sauce
Potato Sauté à Cru
Salad with Garlic Dressing

A CLASSIC EVERYDAY DISH—AND GREAT AS LEFTOVERS, TOO

Pot-au-Feu

Vegetable and Vermicelli Soup
Beef, Turkey, and Mustard Salad

COMFORT FOOD: MEAT AND POTATOES

Carrot and Scallion Salad
Salisbury "Steaks" with Vegetable Sauce
Garlic Mashed Potatoes

DOWN-HOME FAVORITES IN ELEGANT DRESS

Grits and Cheese Soufflé
Braised Pork and Cabbage

GOOD FOR THE SOUL: TWO MENUS WITH A SOUTHERN ACCENT

MENU 1.

Seafood Gumbo
Chicken Livers in Salad
Bread and Raisin Pudding

This menu consists of robust food that not only fills you up but is a real heart warmer for the cold winter months.

The fish and shrimp for the Seafood Gumbo are poached briefly beforehand in boiling water, then removed from the poaching liquid. The remainder of the gumbo ingredients are then cooked in the same poaching liquid, and the poached fish and shrimp are added at the last minute so they don't overcook.

I use codfish here because it is abundant and inexpensive in New England, where I live, although any type of fillet, from catfish to pollack or perch, could be used. I also like to use small fresh or frozen shrimp in my gumbo. One-half pound yields about four shrimp per person, which is sufficient. This dish can be made ahead and refrigerated up to the point of adding the seafood.

Traditionally, the name *gumbo* denotes the presence of okra (also called *gumbo*), and it is included here, although many recent gumbo recipes do not call for it. Another conventional gumbo component and important ingredient in African-based Creole cooking is filé powder, the crushed leaves of the sassafras tree. Authentic New Orleans gumbo usually includes a dark roux made of vegetable oil and flour; the one here is made with canola oil and flour. All three of these ingredients—okra, filé powder, and the dark oil/flour roux—are thickening agents in this fairly spicy dish.

After this heavy first course, a light salad is a welcome follow-up. The main ingredients in the salad are chicken livers, sautéed briefly so they remain pink inside, and iceberg lettuce, which I use because I particularly like its crunchiness. The salad greens are simply tossed with the drippings remaining after the chicken livers are sautéed, some vinegar, and seasonings.

The Bread and Raisin Pudding in this menu is a hearty winter dessert that makes good use of leftover bread. This dish can be made ahead. Thin slices of the leftover bread are toasted in the oven, arranged in a gratin dish, and topped with a mixture of half-and-half, sugar, eggs, vanilla, and raisins before baking.

With this eclectic menu, I would suggest an earthy Zinfandel from California, which would complement the gumbo well.

SEAFOOD GUMBO

There are more ingredients in this recipe than I usually use, but you can eliminate some and/or make substitutions in the fish, shellfish, and vegetables based on market availability. For example, instead of using both fish and shrimp in the gumbo, you can use only one. You could also add some sausage or ham. Especially good choices would be the tasso ham of Louisiana and andouille, a spicy American sausage that is totally different from its French namesake, but very popular in New Orleans.

TOTAL TIME:
1 HOUR

³/₄ *pound fish fillets (pollack, cod, or other fresh fish), cut into 1-inch pieces*

¹/₂ *pound (about 26) small peeled fresh or frozen shrimp (50 to 55 to the pound)*

¹/₄ *cup canola oil*

¹/₃ *cup flour*

2 *onions (about 10 ounces), peeled and sliced (about 2¹/₂ cups)*

¹/₂ *cup long-grain rice*

About 12 scallions, damaged leaves removed and discarded, cut into ¹/₂-inch pieces (about 1 ¹/₂ cups)

5 *cloves garlic, peeled, crushed, and chopped (about 1 tablespoon)*

2 *tomatoes (³/₄ pound), cut into 1-inch pieces (about 2¹/₂ cups)*

1 *cup sliced celery*

1 *green bell pepper (about ¹/₂ pound), seeded and cut into ¹/₂-inch pieces (about 1¹/₂ cups)*

¹/₂ *pound okra, ends trimmed, cut into ¹/₂-inch rounds*

2 *teaspoons salt*

1 *teaspoon dried thyme*

1 *jalapeño pepper, seeded and chopped fine (about 1 tablespoon)*

¹/₄ *teaspoon cayenne pepper*

1 *tablespoon filé gumbo powder*

1. Bring 2 quarts water to a boil in a large stockpot or saucepan. Add the fish and shrimp, stir, and cook over high heat for about 4 minutes.

continued

(The water will not even have returned to the boil by then.) With a slotted spoon, remove the seafood, place it a bowl, cover, and set aside. Reserve the poaching liquid in the pot.

2. Meanwhile, mix the oil and flour together in a small skillet and cook over high heat for about 1 minute, until the mixture sizzles. Reduce the heat to low, and cook for about 15 minutes, stirring every minute or two, until this roux is a deep mahogany color. Add the sliced onions to the mixture and stir well. Then stir the roux and onions into the seafood poaching liquid in the stockpot, and bring to a boil, stirring constantly. Add the rice, and stir well to incorporate it.

3. Add the remainder of the ingredients except the reserved fish and shrimp and the filé powder to the stockpot. Stir, bring the mixture to a boil, reduce the heat to low, cover, and boil gently for 20 minutes. Stir, sprinkle the filé powder on top, mix well, and cook for another 5 minutes.

4. If serving immediately, add the cooked fish and shrimp, return to the boil, and serve. If serving later, set aside to cool, and reheat at serving time, adding the cooked fish and shrimp at the last minute to warm them through.

YIELD: 6 SERVINGS

CHICKEN LIVERS IN SALAD

Easy to prepare and quite refreshing, the salad should be made at the last minute and served while still lukewarm.

TOTAL TIME:
10 MINUTES

12 *whole chicken livers*

1¹/₂ *tablespoons unsalted butter*

5 *tablespoons corn oil*

³/₄ *teaspoon salt*

³/₄ *teaspoon freshly ground black pepper*

4 *cloves garlic, peeled, crushed, and chopped (about 1 tablespoon)*

3 *tablespoons coarsely chopped parsley, preferably the flat-leaf variety*

6 *cups large dice (1-inch) iceberg lettuce*

3 *tablespoons red wine vinegar*

1. Wash the chicken livers under cool water and separate them into halves, cutting out and discarding the connecting sinew.

2. Heat the butter and 2 tablespoons of the oil until very hot in one very large (12-inch) saucepan or two smaller pans. Add the chicken livers in one layer, sprinkle them with half the salt and pepper, and sauté over high heat for 1 minute, covering the pan partially with a lid if splattering occurs. Turn and cook the livers on the other side for 1 minute, partially covering the pan again if necessary to avoid splattering. (The livers should be pink inside.)

3. Add the garlic and parsley and mix well. With a slotted spoon, transfer the livers to a bowl, cover, and set aside.

4. Place the diced lettuce in a large serving bowl. Add the chicken liver pan drippings to the lettuce and toss to mix well. Add the remainder of the salt and pepper and the vinegar, and mix again.

5. Divide the salad among six individual plates, serving 4 liver halves per person. Serve immediately, while still lukewarm.

YIELD: 6 SERVINGS

continued

BREAD AND RAISIN PUDDING

TOTAL TIME:
1 HOUR

This is a great vehicle for leftover bread, but if you have leftover rolls, cake, or even Danish pastries on hand, use them instead, slicing and toasting them first as you would the bread.

4 *ounces thinly sliced (¹/4-inch) bread, preferably from a crusty country loaf, lightly toasted in the oven or toaster*

1 *cup golden raisins*

4 *large eggs*

3 *cups half-and-half*

¹/2 *cup granulated sugar*

2 *teaspoons vanilla*

1 *teaspoon confectioner's sugar*

1. Arrange the toasted bread slices in the bottom of a 6-cup gratin dish so they completely cover the bottom. Top with the raisins.

2. Beat the eggs in a bowl, and mix in the half-and-half, granulated sugar, and vanilla. Pour evenly over the bread so that all the slices are moistened.

3. Place the gratin dish in a preheated 375-degree oven and bake for 40 minutes, or until set. Cool.

4. At serving time, sprinkle with the confectioner's sugar. Serve cool, but not cold.

YIELD: 6 SERVINGS

∂

MENU 2.

Celery and Apple Salad
Black-eyed Peas and Kale Ragout
Hot Wine
Cozy Cider

D ried beans are one of the best buys for creating those soul-warming, nutritious dishes that we all crave in the winter. Not only are they high in protein, vitamins, and fiber, but with prices constantly escalating at the supermarket, they are one of the least-expensive, highest-yielding foods.

There are a great many varieties of dried beans available, from black to white to red kidney. The ragout recipe here uses black-eyed peas, those little oval beans with a black dot in the middle. Wash the beans thoroughly, removing any damaged specimens or foreign material, but don't soak them any longer than an hour, unless you know they are several years old.

In this Southern-inspired recipe, I use pieces of the rind and fat from a Virginia ham. I occasionally buy the ham whole, slicing and serving it like prosciutto. After I trim the ham for serving, I freeze the pieces of rind and fat that I removed so I will have them on hand for dishes like this. If you don't have any ham trimmings, use the lean, unsalted rolled bacon called *pancetta* in Italian and *lard salé* in French. If these are too expensive, use regular bacon.

continued

I cook the beans and greens separately for the ragout. Although I use kale here, collard greens work just as well, especially when small and tender ones are available, as do turnip greens, Swiss chard, or spinach. The kale can, of course, be served on its own, as can the beans, seasoned lightly with a little salt, pepper, and oil. I combine them here and cook them together briefly for this rich, earthy, comforting main dish, served with Tabasco on the side.

A zesty forerunner to the black-eyed peas is a salad made of celery and apples in a mixture of sour cream and lemon juice. If possible, use the tender, pale green inside ribs of celery, cutting them into thin julienne strips. If you do use the darker, tougher exterior ribs of the celery, be sure to peel the outsides with a vegetable peeler to remove the fibrous skin before proceeding with the recipe.

The hot cider is best made with cloudy, unfiltered sweet cider, the fresh juice of pressed apples, which is then combined with cloves, allspice berries, and stick cinnamon. After being steeped together in the cider, the cloves and allspice come to the top and can be removed before serving, and the stick of cinnamon, which sinks to the bottom, can be served with the liquid. I add a little bourbon to this concoction, but that is optional.

I am also including a recipe for hot wine, another appealing cold-weather drink traditionally prepared in the French countryside. This drink is best made with a fruity, acidic wine, like a Beaujolais, or a heavier wine like a Zinfandel. The wine is heated almost to the boil, sweetened with sugar, and served with a fresh wedge of lemon.

CELERY AND APPLE SALAD

The sweetness of the apples is offset nicely by the mildly acidic combination of sour cream and lemon juice. Don't peel the apples; along with the celery, the apple skin lends texture to the dish.

TOTAL TIME: 15 MINUTES

6 *ribs celery (about 8 ounces), as pale green and tender as possible*

2 *medium Red Delicious apples (about 12 ounces)*

1¹/₂ *tablespoons lemon juice*

¹/₂ *cup sour cream*

³/₄ *teaspoon freshly ground black pepper*

¹/₂ *teaspoon salt*

1 *teaspoon sugar*

6 *lettuce leaves, for garnish*

1. Trim the celery ribs to remove the leaves (reserve the trimmings for stock), and peel the ribs with a vegetable peeler if the outer surface is tough or fibrous. Wash and cut the ribs into 2-inch pieces. Then press the pieces flat on the table and cut them lengthwise into thin strips. You should have about 2¹/₂ cups. Place them in a bowl.

2. Since the apples are not peeled for this recipe, wash them thoroughly in warm water, scraping them lightly with a sharp knife if necessary to remove any surface wax. Stand the apples upright on the table, and cut each one vertically into ¹/₂-inch-thick slices, stopping when you reach the core, pivoting the apple, and cutting again, until only the core remains. Then discard the cores, stack the apple slices together, and cut them into ¹/₂-inch strips. Add the strips to the celery with all the remaining ingredients except the lettuce leaves, and mix well.

3. To serve, arrange the lettuce leaves on six individual plates, and spoon the salad onto the leaves.

YIELD: 6 SERVINGS

BLACK-EYED PEAS AND
KALE RAGOUT

TOTAL TIME:
1 HOUR

Generally recipes tell you to soak dried beans overnight, but I don't advise it; it may actually have an adverse effect on the beans. After a night of soaking, the water is often full of bubbles, indicating fermentation. Instead of soaking, cover the beans with cold water and put them on to cook with a dash of salt. The black-eyed peas I cooked the last time I made this ragout were tender after forty-five minutes of cooking. Although some slightly older varieties may take longer, they shouldn't require more than one and a half hours to cook.

1 *pound dried black-eyed peas (see Note)*

1 *teaspoon salt*

1 *jalapeño pepper, seeded and coarsely chopped (about*
   1 tablespoon) (optional)

8 *ounces rind and trimmings from Virginia ham, pancetta, or*
   bacon, cut into ³/₄-inch pieces

2 *onions (about 8 ounces), peeled and cut into 1-inch pieces*

4 *cloves garlic, peeled and sliced (about 2 tablespoons)*

1¹/₂ *pounds kale, collard greens, or spinach, leaves cut into*
   2-inch pieces and stems into ¹/₂-inch pieces

Tabasco sauce (optional)

1. Wash the peas and remove and discard any damaged ones or foreign material. Place the peas in a pot with 6 cups cold water, the salt, and jalapeño pepper, if desired. Bring to a boil, reduce the heat to very low, cover, and cook for 45 minutes, or until tender. Most of the liquid will have been absorbed by the peas.

2. Meanwhile, place the pieces of ham in a saucepan and cook over low to medium heat until the fat is rendered and the ham is browned on all sides, about 10 minutes. Add the onions and garlic, and sauté for about 1 minute.

3. Wash the kale carefully under cool water, and add it, still wet from washing, to the ham in the saucepan. Press down on the kale to fit it in the pan, cover, and cook until wilted and soft, about 10 minutes. (If substituting collard greens or spinach for kale, don't cook them as long; the spinach, for example, will be tender in about 1 minute.)

4. At serving time, add the kale mixture to the beans, stir, bring to a boil, and simmer for 8 to 10 minutes. Serve with the Tabasco sauce, if desired.

NOTE: If you cook the dried peas ahead for the ragout, you will notice that they tend to dry out if left to stand for a few hours or longer. Add ½ cup water to the peas and bring them to a boil before adding the kale mixture. Stir, return to a boil, and simmer 5 to 10 minutes before serving.

YIELD: 6 SERVINGS

HOT WINE

This warming drink is a favorite of farmers in the Beaujolais area of Burgundy, where I come from.

TOTAL TIME:
6 TO 8 MINUTES

6 *cups (about 2 bottles) robust, fruity, acidic wine (Beaujolais, Cabernet Sauvignon, Merlot, or Zinfandel)*

½ *cup sugar*

1 *large lemon, cut into 6 wedges*

1. Place the wine in a saucepan with the sugar and heat the mixture slowly until just below a boil. Meanwhile, squeeze the juice from 1 wedge of the lemon into each of six mugs and drop the wedges into the mugs.

2. Divide the wine among the mugs, and serve immediately.

YIELD: 6 SERVINGS

COZY CIDER

TOTAL TIME:
10 MINUTES
I call this drink my New England cold remedy; it's my prescription for getting rid of a stuffy nose or a sore throat.

1½ *quarts unfiltered sweet cider*
12 *allspice berries*
12 *whole cloves*
2 *sticks cinnamon, broken into pieces*
6 *tablespoons bourbon (optional)*

1. Place all the ingredients but the bourbon in a saucepan and heat over medium heat until the mixture is just below the boil. Cover, remove from the heat, and let steep for 5 minutes.

2. At that point, the allspice and cloves will have floated to the top; remove and discard them. Pour a tablespoon of bourbon, if desired, into each of six mugs and pour some of the cider mixture over it. Spoon a few cinnamon stick pieces into each mug, and serve immediately.

YIELD: 6 SERVINGS

COMFORTING FOOD FOR
A COLD WINTER DAY

Pumpkin and Pastina Soup
Squid à l'Ail
Carrot and Sunflower Seed Salad

At any time of the year, but never more so than on a cold winter day, soup is the first and foremost comforting food for me. It can be made ahead, it enables you to use the leftover vegetables and meat in the refrigerator, and it is an ideal vehicle for seasonal vegetables like pumpkin.

Pumpkin, quite inexpensive in the winter months, is often sold in large pieces at the supermarket. Not only do I prepare gratins with it, but I love to use it in soups; it has a smooth and creamy texture, and is a beautiful orange color when cooked. I combine it here with pastina (small pasta that comes in shapes that range from little dots to rings to alphabet letters.)

For a main dish, squid is one of the least expensive and most delicious seafoods on the market and its preparation entails almost no trimming or waste. It is available fresh almost year-round in fish stores and is also sold frozen—sometimes cleaned and ready to use—in supermarkets.

Although the squid can be sautéed as is, it will be more tender if you blanch it briefly in boiling water before sautéeing it at the last moment and combining it with the seasonings.

continued

The salad in this menu is a wonderfully crunchy-textured one: carrots combined with sunflower seeds, available in supermarkets or health food stores, accented with cider vinegar.

With this menu, try beer or cider (especially a hard variety) instead of wine.

SPECIAL TIP   ROASTED PUMPKIN SEEDS: *When cleaning a pumpkin, remove the seeds, rinse them under cool water, and pat them dry. Then spread the seeds out on a baking sheet and place them in a 350-degree oven for about 30 minutes, until lightly browned on top.*

For each cup of seeds, heat 1 tablespoon unsalted butter in a skillet, and mix in a pinch of cayenne pepper and ⅛ teaspoon salt. Add the seeds and stir to coat them thoroughly.

These make a terrific snack with drinks, and are also good sprinkled on a bowl of soup. Eat shell and all, or discard the tougher pieces of shell and eat the remainder along with the green nuts inside.

PUMPKIN AND PASTINA SOUP

TOTAL TIME:
1 HOUR

This recipe combines creamy pumpkin with the small pasta called pastina, but if you prefer, you can use another member of the pasta family, from tiny noodles to small elbows to broken pieces of spaghetti, in this delicate but hearty soup.

1 *leek (about 8 ounces), dark green outer leaves and any damaged or wilted inner leaves removed and discarded*

1 *tablespoon unsalted butter*

1 *tablespoon corn oil*

1 *piece ripe pumpkin (about 2¼ pounds)*

2 *cups chicken stock or 2 bouillon cubes dissolved in 2 cups water*

Salt to taste (about ½ teaspoon)

½ *cup pastina*

1. Split the leek lengthwise into quarters and then cut it (both green and white parts) crosswise into thin slices. Transfer the slices to a bowl and wash them thoroughly in cool water. Lift the slices from the bowl and place them in a large pot with the butter and oil. Sauté over high heat for 2 to 3 minutes, until the leek begins to sizzle lightly.

2. Meanwhile, with a sharp knife, carefully peel the tough outer skin from the pumpkin. You should have about 1½ pounds of pumpkin flesh. Remove and reserve the seeds (see the Special Tip, page 204) and cut the flesh into ½-inch pieces. You should have about 5½ cups.

3. Add the cubed pumpkin, the chicken stock, 4 cups water, and salt to taste to the leeks in the pot, and bring the mixture to a boil. Cover, reduce the heat, and cook at a gentle boil for 30 minutes.

4. Add the pastina and cook for 10 minutes longer. Stir and serve immediately.

YIELD: 6 SERVINGS

SQUID A L'AIL

TOTAL TIME:
10 MINUTES
(IF THE SQUID
IS ALREADY
CLEANED)

If the squid you buy requires cleaning, allow it to defrost slowly under refrigeration if frozen. To clean, remove the blackish skin from the outside, then open the body and remove and discard the pen (the translucent central cartilage bone). Cut off the tentacles at the head and eyes and press on the round part where the tentacles come together. A knotty beak will come out of the center. Discard it. Wash the squid thoroughly under cool water.

2   pounds squid, thoroughly cleaned

3   tablespoons olive oil

1$^1/_2$ tablespoons unsalted butter

14 or 15   scallions, green tips and damaged leaves removed and discarded, cut into 1-inch pieces (about 2$^1/_4$ cups)

$^3/_4$ teaspoon salt

$^3/_4$ teaspoon freshly ground black pepper

3 to 4   cloves garlic, chopped (about 1$^1/_2$ teaspoons)

3   tablespoons chopped parsley

1. Bring 4 cups water to a boil in a saucepan. Meanwhile, cut the body of the squid lengthwise into $^1/_2$-inch strips and the tentacles into pieces. When the water is boiling, drop the squid into the water and cook it for 30 seconds (the water will not return to the boil). Drain in a colander, and set aside.

2. At serving time, divide the oil and butter equally between two skillets, and place the skillets over high heat. When very hot, add the scallions and sauté for about 10 seconds. Then add the squid, salt, and pepper, and sauté over high heat for 2 to 3 minutes. Mix in the garlic and parsley. Divide among six plates, and serve immediately.

YIELD: 6 SERVINGS

CARROT AND SUNFLOWER
SEED SALAD

This dish can be served as a first course as well as a salad, and is also good as a sandwich filling, either on its own or with cold cuts.

6   medium-size carrots (about 12 ounces)

1/2   cup sunflower seeds

4   cloves garlic, peeled, crushed, and chopped (about 2 teaspoons)

2   scallions, finely minced (about 1/4 cup)

1   teaspoon freshly ground black pepper

1/2   teaspoon salt

2   tablespoons cider vinegar

5   tablespoons corn oil

6   leaves lettuce, for garnish

1. Trim the carrots at both ends, peel them with a vegetable peeler, and shred them, using either a conventional cheese grater (large holes) or a food processor fitted with the grater attachment.

2. Combine the carrot strips with the sunflower seeds, garlic, scallions, pepper, salt, cider vinegar, and oil in a bowl. Mix well and serve on the lettuce leaves.

YIELD: 6 SERVINGS

HEARTY FARE IN
AN ORIENTAL MOOD

Bread and Onion Pancakes
Sautéed Soy Chicken
Baked Yams

Here are three robust dishes seasoned in the Oriental manner that are guaranteed to keep you warm and satisfied on even the worst winter day.

Bread and Onion Pancakes are served as a first course, although they would be equally good for brunch, breakfast, or as a light lunch with a salad. Simple, delicious, and filling, they're a big moneysaver, as you make them with leftover bread.

The seasonings for the Sautéed Soy Chicken are similar to those used in the pancake sauce, repeating the Oriental theme. A large chicken is divided into six pieces to yield portions that are not very large, but are still substantial enough since the pancake first course and the baked yam dish are quite filling.

I remove the skin from the chicken, eliminating a great deal of the fat and therefore a lot of calories; the chicken cooks much faster without it and will still be tender and moist. The chicken can be sautéed ahead, but if you do so, don't add the scallions, tomatoes, and chicken liver until you reheat the dish at the last minute, or they will overcook.

continued

You can use yellow sweet potatoes or red sweet potatoes, called yams, for the Baked Yams. The orangey-red yams are a favorite at my house and we like them best baked in the oven. The skin, which contains most of the vitamins, is edible. Be sure, however, to cut out and discard any damaged spots visible on the skin, and trim the yams at either end or prick them to provide an outlet for the steam and so prevent them from bursting.

As a light finish to this filling meal, I suggest fresh fruit for dessert. Try a Connecticut Pinot Noir with this menu as a daring departure from California wines. There are good ones from Crosswoods and Chamart that are unusual, delightful, and well priced.

BREAD AND ONION PANCAKES

These pancakes are served with a spicy sauce containing vinegar, soy sauce, ginger, Tabasco, and garlic, but they are good without the sauce, too, and either way make a very good accompaniment to a roast or a baked chicken. I like mine small, with crisp edges, but you can make yours larger if you prefer.

TOTAL TIME:
40 MINUTES

FOR THE BATTER

10 *ounces bread, preferably coarse textured, cut into 1-inch cubes (about 8 to 10 cups)*

2 *cups chicken stock or broth*

1½ *cups chopped onion*

⅓ *cup minced coriander (cilantro) or parsley, loosely packed*

½ *teaspoon Tabasco sauce*

4 *large eggs*

½ *teaspoon salt*

FOR THE SAUCE

¼ *cup red wine vinegar*

¼ *cup soy sauce*

1 *teaspoon sugar*

½ *teaspoon ground ginger*

½ *teaspoon hot oil or Tabasco sauce*

4 *cloves garlic, peeled, crushed, and chopped (about 2 teaspoons)*

1 *tablespoon corn oil*

½ *cup peanut or corn oil*

1. *For the batter:* Crush the bread cubes into the chicken stock in a mixing bowl. Add the remaining batter ingredients and crush with your hands, kneading the mixture until it is well blended but not completely smooth; there should still be small visible lumps of wet bread.

2. *For the sauce:* Mix all the sauce ingredients together in a bowl. Set aside.

continued

CUISINE ECONOMIQUE / 211

3. Heat 1 ½ tablespoons of the oil in a large, nonstick skillet. When hot, add about ⅓ cup of the pancake mixture to the skillet, spreading it with a spoon into a disk about 4 inches in diameter and about ⅜ inch thick. Repeat, working quickly, to shape 2 or 3 more pancakes (depending on the size of your skillet), and cook over medium to high heat for about 4 minutes. Then, turn and cook the pancakes for 4 minutes on the other side.

4. Transfer the pancakes to an ovenproof plate and place in a warm oven (140 to 150 degrees) while you continue making pancakes with the remaining batter and oil. (Although the pancakes are best eaten immediately after cooking, they can be cooked ahead, cooled, and then reheated under a hot broiler just before serving.)

5. Serve warm, with the sauce.

YIELD: 16 PANCAKES

*S*PECIAL TIP   FRUIT PANCAKES: *For a variation, soak the bread in milk instead of chicken stock, eliminate the onion, coriander, Tabasco, and salt, and add diced apple or pieces of another fruit you have on hand along with a little sugar to the batter. (Omit the sauce.) Cook these fruit pancakes in the same way as indicated in the recipe and serve them for breakfast with a little maple syrup or a dusting of sugar.*

SAUTÉED SOY CHICKEN

Instead of buying a whole chicken for this dish, you can buy six chicken legs and prepare them in the same manner.

TOTAL TIME:
45 MINUTES

1 *4-pound chicken*

2 *tablespoons peanut or corn oil*

1 *tablespoon dark soy sauce*

$^1/_2$ *teaspoon Tabasco sauce*

12 *scallions, damaged leaves removed and discarded, cut into 1-inch pieces (about 1 $^1/_2$ cups)*

18 *cherry tomatoes*

$^1/_4$ *teaspoon salt*

$^1/_4$ *teaspoon freshly ground black pepper*

1. Remove the legs from the chicken and pull off all their skin. Cut each leg into 2 pieces, separating the drumstick from the thigh. Set the pieces aside. Cut the 2 wings from the chicken at the shoulder joints and set them aside. Pull off the skin from the chicken breasts and carcass and remove the 2 breasts. Set them aside. Freeze the chicken neck and carcass bones for use in stock and either discard the skin or spread it out on a cookie sheet and cook it in a 400-degree oven for 20 to 25 minutes, until crisp, for crackling to crumble over salads or soups.

2. Place the chicken drumsticks, thighs, breasts, wings, gizzard, and liver in a dish and add the oil, soy sauce, and Tabasco sauce. Mix well and let macerate until cooking time. (The recipe can be completed to this point up to 1 day ahead. Refrigerate the chicken breasts and the chicken in the marinade.)

3. Transfer the drumsticks, thighs, wings, and gizzard to a large nonstick skillet (reserving the marinade), and cook them, covered, over medium heat for about 12 minutes, turning the pieces occasionally so they brown uniformly on all sides. Add the chicken breasts and cook, covered, for an additional 6 to 7 minutes, turning the breasts after about 3 minutes. Remove the skillet from the heat and set the chicken aside, covered, until serving time. (Although it is preferable to cook the dish just before serving, it can be prepared through this step up to 30 minutes before serving.)

continued

4. Just before serving, add the scallions, tomatoes, the reserved marinade, 2 tablespoons water, the chicken liver (halved), salt, and pepper to the chicken. Cook, covered, for 2½ to 3 minutes.

5. Divide the 4 pieces of dark meat and the 2 wings among six plates. Cut each of the breasts into 3 pieces and add a piece of breast meat to each plate with a small piece of the liver. Spoon some of the tomatoes and sauce over the chicken and serve with the Baked Yams.

YIELD: 6 SERVINGS

BAKED YAMS

TOTAL TIME:
50 MINUTES

Placing these potatoes on an aluminum foil–lined cookie sheet will help them cook faster and eliminate time-consuming clean-up chores, but do not wrap them in aluminum foil: They lose their delicious crisp skin and become wet and soggy throughout when wrapped.

6 *yams (red sweet potatoes), about 8 ounces each*

1. Remove any dark spots or damaged areas from the yams and wash them thoroughly under cool water.

2. If you did not have to cut out any damaged areas from the potatoes, trim them at either end or prick them to allow steam to escape. Place the potatoes on a foil-lined cookie sheet and bake them in a preheated 400-degree oven for about 50 minutes, until soft and tender.

3. Serve immediately.

YIELD: 6 SERVINGS

FOR THE ADVENTUROUS GOURMET

Chicken Hearts and Gizzards Soup
Catfish with Croutons and Nuts
Pears in Mint and Tea

ಿ

Having grown up in a part of France—Bourg-en-Bresse—famous for its chickens at a time when money and food were scarce, I am conditioned to making use of all the parts of the bird.

The flavorful and filling Chicken Hearts and Gizzards Soup that starts this menu is an example of this thriftiness. Although it is a first course here, it would also be good on its own with a salad and a piece of cheese as a light supper.

Both gizzards and hearts are usually available inexpensively in pack-ages, either fresh or frozen, in most supermarkets. They are quite tasty and good textured, provided they are cooked long enough to become tender.

Flavored with scallions and carrots, the soup is finished with a garnish of sour cream and a sprinkling of cilantro leaves, which gives it a Jewish/Russian flavor. The sour cream and cilantro can be omitted for a plainer, less sophisticated result.

The main dish features catfish, which is now farm raised and available almost year-round from most fishmongers, garnished with walnuts and croutons. Use leftover French bread, if possible, for the croûtons; it has a chewier texture when sautéed than regular white bread.

For dessert, pears are flavored with a packet of regular tea and shredded fresh mint, which is usually in markets year-round across the country. If it isn't available or is too expensive, add a package of mint-flavored herb tea to obtain the desired flavor.

A Spanish white wine from Torres, usually reasonably priced, would go well with the catfish.

CHICKEN HEARTS AND GIZZARDS SOUP

TOTAL TIME:
2 HOURS AND
15 MINUTES

Notice that the gizzards are first cooked whole for forty-five minutes before being cut into pieces; they are difficult to cut raw, as they are rubbery and tough and tend to slip under the knife. ·

Cornmeal is the thickening agent in the soup, but farina, semolina, couscous, oatmeal, or the like can be substituted.

2 *pounds chicken gizzards and hearts or gizzards only*

2 TO 4 *ribs celery (about 7 ounces), cut into ¹/₂-inch pieces (about 2 cups)*

4 *medium carrots (about 10 ounces), peeled and cut into ¹/₂-inch pieces (about 2 cups)*

1¹/₂ *teaspoons salt*

¹/₃ *cup yellow cornmeal*

8 *scallions, dark green and damaged or wilted outer leaves removed and discarded, coarsely chopped (1 ¹/₄ cups)*

¹/₂ *teaspoon dried dill weed*

¹/₂ *cup sour cream, for garnish (optional)*

¹/₄ *cup loosely packed cilantro (coriander) leaves, for garnish (optional)*

1. Wash the gizzards and hearts under cool running water. Place them in a saucepan with 6 cups water, and bring to a boil over high heat. Boil for 1 to 2 minutes and then skim off and discard any fat and impurities that rise to the surface. Cover, reduce the heat to low, and boil gently for 45 minutes.

2. With a slotted spoon, remove the gizzards and hearts from the cooking liquid and place them on a chopping board. When cool enough to handle, cut them into ¼-inch pieces, or chop them coarsely in a food processor. Return them to the cooking liquid with the celery, carrots, and salt. Bring back to a boil over high heat, cover, reduce the heat to low, and boil gently for another 45 minutes.

3. Stir in the cornmeal, scallions, and dill, and cook for 15 minutes longer, stirring occasionally.

4. Spoon into bowls. Garnish, if desired, with a tablespoon of the sour cream and a sprinkling of the cilantro.

YIELD: 6 SERVINGS

CATFISH WITH CROUTONS AND NUTS

TOTAL TIME:
10 TO 15
MINUTES

If you can't find catfish, use the freshest, least expensive fish instead, perhaps scrod or cod, both of which are usually reasonably priced.

If you don't want to bone the catfish yourself, buy it already filleted. The skin will have been removed, but, holding your knife almost horizontal to the fish, cut off some of the underlying white fatty tissue from the surface of the flesh. Particularly evident on larger catfish, this tissue tends to have a strong flavor.

3 tablespoons canola or sunflower oil

A piece of French bread (about 2 ounces), cut into $^{1}/_{2}$-inch cubes (about 1$^{1}/_{2}$ cups)

$^{1}/_{2}$ cup walnut (or another variety of nut) pieces

2 tablespoons unsalted butter

2 tablespoons virgin olive oil

6 catfish fillets (6 to 8 ounces each), skin removed and some of the underlying white fatty tissue cut off

$^{1}/_{2}$ teaspoon salt

$^{1}/_{2}$ teaspoon freshly ground black pepper

4 cloves garlic, peeled, crushed, and chopped fine (about 1 tablespoon)

$^{1}/_{4}$ cup chopped chives or parsley

Red wine vinegar (optional)

1. Heat the canola oil in a large skillet. When hot, add the bread cubes and nuts and sauté them for about 4 minutes, until nicely browned on all sides. Transfer to a plate.

2. Heat the butter and olive oil in the same skillet. Sprinkle the fish fillets on both sides with the salt and pepper, and place them in one layer in the skillet. Sauté 1$^{1}/_{2}$ minutes on each side, until the fish is just cooked in the center.

3. Arrange the catfish on a platter or divide it among individual plates. Add the garlic and chives to the drippings in the skillet and cook for about 15 seconds. Then, add $^{1}/_{4}$ cup water to the skillet and stir to dissolve all the solidified bits in the bottom of the pan.

4. To serve, pour the resulting pan sauce over the fish, spoon on the croutons and nuts, and serve immediately, sprinkling the fish, if desired, with a little red wine vinegar.

YIELD: 6 SERVINGS

Pears in Mint and Tea

TOTAL TIME:
30 MINUTES
PLUS
COOLING TIME

In winter, I usually use Bosc pears, which are not too expensive and lend themselves well to long cooking, for this dish. It took twenty minutes for the wedges of pear to cook when I last prepared this recipe, but they may be tender in half the time if very ripe or they may take up to forty minutes to cook if they are less ripe. Test them occasionally as they cook with the point of a knife or a fork. Remove them from the heat as soon as they are tender and let them cool in their own juices.

1 *large lemon*

¹/₂ *cup sugar*

6 *Bosc pears (about 2 pounds)*

1 *regular tea bag (orange pekoe or another tea to your liking)*

¹/₃ *cup shredded fresh mint leaves or 1 mint-flavored herb tea bag*

1 *teaspoon cornstarch dissolved in 2 teaspoons water*

1. Pour 2 cups water into a stainless steel saucepan. With a vegetable peeler, peel the surface of the lemon, removing long strips of peel. Cut the lemon in half and press it to extract the juice. You should have 2 to 3 tablespoons of lemon juice. Add the lemon peel and juice to the water with the sugar and mix to combine.

2. Peel the pears and cut them into quarters. Remove the cores and place the pear wedges in the saucepan. Add the ordinary tea bag and, if fresh mint is not available, the mint-flavored tea bag. Bring the mixture to a boil over high heat, cover, reduce the heat to low and cook gently for about 20 minutes, until the pear pieces are tender when pierced with the point of a knife or with a fork. Remove from the heat.

3. Immediately add the dissolved cornstarch to the saucepan and stir it into the juices to thicken them slightly. Let the pears cool in the syrup.

4. When ready to serve, remove the tea bag(s) and discard them. If using fresh mint, stir it gently into the syrup. Divide the pears among six plates (4 wedges per plate). Spoon some of the syrup over the pears and serve.

YIELD: 6 SERVINGS

DO-AHEAD DISHES
FOR BUSY DAYS

Cauliflower Soup
Lamb and Yams Fricassee
Apple Stew

For busy times before the holidays, I like to prepare some dishes ahead and refrigerate them to have on hand. They are perfect for days when I come home late, as they can be reheated and ready to serve in minutes.

This menu uses seasonal ingredients, the best choice for economy and quality. The Cauliflower Soup is simple and straightforward. I use a little flour as a thickening agent, although potatoes, couscous, or another starch could be substituted. Since cauliflower doesn't have a pronounced flavor, curry powder gives the soup the accent it needs.

The lamb pieces in the fricassee are a combination of meat and bones, usually from the neck or shoulder; they are quite inexpensive and very meaty. This is a casual dish: The bones are picked up at the table and the meat eaten directly from them.

For the Apple Stew, many apple varieties are available during the winter months. Try to choose a fairly acidic, soft apple (Macoun, McIntosh, or Rome Beauty), although you can use the least expensive of these because any apple will work.

This winter menu is good with a cool, robust Chianti. Such a wine usually carries a good price for its quality.

CAULIFLOWER SOUP

TOTAL TIME:
50 MINUTES

This is one of those wonderful dishes that can be made ahead and frozen, or it can be refrigerated for a few days and reheated as needed.

2 tablespoons canola oil

2 onions (about 10 ounces), peeled and quartered

2 tablespoons flour

1 teaspoon curry powder

2 cups homemade chicken stock or canned chicken broth

1 teaspoon salt (or more or less depending on the saltiness of the stock)

1/2 teaspoon freshly ground black pepper

1 large or 2 small heads cauliflower (about 1 3/4 pounds total, or 1 1/2 pounds cleaned), separated into flowerets, trimmed, and cleaned (see Note)

2 tablespoons unsalted butter

1. Heat the oil in a saucepan. When hot, add the onions and sauté for 2 to 3 minutes, until they start browning. Sprinkle the flour and curry powder over the onions and mix well.

2. Stir in the chicken stock, 2 cups water, the salt, and pepper. Mix well and bring to a boil, stirring occasionally. Add the cauliflower, return to the boil, cover, reduce the heat to very low, and boil gently for 30 minutes. (At this point, the dish could be served with the cauliflower pieces broken into slightly smaller pieces rather than pureed.)

3. Drain the liquid from the soup into a mixing bowl. Place the solids with a little of the liquid (too much will make the soup foamy) in the bowl of a food processor. Process until smooth, then combine with the reserved liquid. You should have about 7 cups of soup. If you have less, add enough boiling water to bring it to this level. Stir in the butter until melted.

4. Divide the soup among six soup dishes, and serve immediately.

NOTE: The cauliflower stems and most of the attached root section are usable in this recipe.

YIELD: 6 SERVINGS

LAMB AND YAMS FRICASSEE

TOTAL TIME:
1 HOUR AND 30
MINUTES

I use yams in the lamb fricassee because I like their bright orange color, but paler sweet potatoes can be substituted. So can butternut or acorn squash, or rutabagas, if they are a deep gold, smooth skinned, and firm.

Select lamb that is as lean as possible, and trim the pieces to remove any remaining exterior fat. Cook the lamb slowly, so the fat is rendered and the meat browns in it without any additional fat. Add a few tablespoons of water occasionally to keep the natural juices in the meat, and skim off any excess fat from the juices at the end of cooking. The fricassee can be cooked ahead and reheated on top of the stove or in a microwave oven.

2½ *pounds lamb pieces, meat and bones, from the neck or shoulder (about 16 pieces)*

3 *pounds yams, peeled*

1 *teaspoon salt*

1 *teaspoon freshly ground black pepper*

1 *teaspoon herbes de Provence (see Note, page 150)*

2 *tablespoons red wine vinegar*

1. Trim off any excess fat from the surface of the lamb pieces and arrange them in one layer in a large heavy casserole or sauté pan. Put the pan over low heat and brown the lamb for approximately 20 minutes, turning the pieces to brown them evenly on all sides.

2. Meanwhile, cut the yams into 3-inch cubes.

3. Add the yams with the remaining ingredients and ⅔ cup water to the pan of lamb. Cook over high heat for 2 minutes. Cover, reduce the heat to very low, and cook for 1 hour, adding a few tablespoons of water as needed if all the moisture disappears. Skim off the surface fat.

4. Serve immediately with the natural juices.

YIELD: 6 SERVINGS

APPLE STEW

I don't peel the apples for this dish because the cooked skin gives it a wonderfully chewy quality. It is excellent with a little sour cream or yogurt, and, if you wish, cookies.

6 *soft apples (Macoun, McIntosh, Rome Beauty) (about 2 pounds)*

²/₃ *cup apricot (or another variety) preserves*

1 *tablespoon unsalted butter*

¹/₄ *cup walnut pieces*

¹/₂ *cup sour cream or plain yogurt*

1. Wash the apples in warm water, scraping them lightly with a sharp knife to remove any wax. Cut into quarters and core.

2. Put the apple pieces in a saucepan with the preserves, ²/₃ cup water, the butter, and walnuts. Bring to a boil, cover, reduce the heat, and cook over low heat for 30 minutes, or until the apples are tender. Cool.

3. Divide among six dessert dishes and serve cold with the sour cream or yogurt on top.

YIELD: 6 SERVINGS

SPECIAL TIP   APPLESAUCE: *For a delicious applesauce, process the apple stew (with or without the walnuts) in a food processor until smooth. Serve with roast pork, duck, or goose.*

BUDGET-MINDED COMPANY FARE

Grilled Eggplant Oriental
Veal Tendrons and Tarragon Sauce
Potato Sauté à Cru
Salad with Garlic Dressing

ә

Veal is one of the most delicate of meats and is the best to prepare in sauces. Prime cuts, like the rack and fillet, are expensive, but in the shoulder, flank, breast, and shank, you can find delicious veal for very little money.

When I was a child, I did not know that veal loin and chops even existed. The standard veal dishes served at our house were veal roast from the shoulder, braised breast of veal, and veal tendrons in creamy tarragon sauce.

I still consider the ribs from the breast of veal, used in the following recipe, to be one of the tastiest cuts. I particularly enjoy serving this dish at family meals, where no one hesitates to pick up the ribs and chew the meat from the bones.

Ribs from the veal breast are available inexpensively in supermarkets. Slowly cooked in a Dutch oven or cast-iron cocotte, they become tender and create a most delectable sauce. This recipe is also excellent made with veal from the shank or shoulder, although it costs more.

continued

The side dish is potatoes *sauté à cru,* which means "sautéed raw."
The cooking method gives the dish a different flavor from that of hash-
brown potatoes, which are made with cooked potatoes. The potatoes can be
peeled, sliced, and placed in water ahead of time, but they taste best if
cooked at the last moment.

Occasionally, when I long for a taste of summer on a cold winter day,
I fire up my barbecue grill and cook something outside. The Grilled Eggplant Oriental that starts this meal is particularly good when the eggplant is
cooked outside on the barbecue. If a grill is not available, however, or you'd
rather not venture out into the cold, the eggplants can be cooked in a heavy
skillet on top of the stove over very high heat.

The dressing for the eggplant, made of soy sauce and rice vinegar, can
also be used on steamed or poached fish or even as a dressing for a green
salad.

For the salad to complete this meal, select curly chicory with a large,
thick heart and very white inner leaves, indicating tenderness. Other salad
greens can be substituted if escarole is not available or is of poor quality.
Toss the salad just before serving with the dressing and serve cool but not
ice cold.

A light red or full-bodied white wine will go well with this menu and,
to finish the meal, I suggest a piece of cheese and a pear.

GRILLED EGGPLANT ORIENTAL

This dish can be made ahead and will keep, refrigerated, for several days, although it should be brought to room temperature or reheated briefly in a microwave oven before serving. It works equally well as a salad course or as an accompaniment for broiled or grilled fish or meat.

TOTAL TIME:
20 TO 22
MINUTES

6 *small eggplants (about 3 ounces each, 1 1/4 pounds total)*
2 *tablespoons canola or safflower oil*
1/4 *teaspoon salt*

FOR THE DRESSING
2 *tablespoons dark soy sauce*
2 *teaspoons rice vinegar*
1/2 *teaspoon sugar*
2 *tablespoons vegetable oil*
1 *tablespoon minced chives, for garnish*

1. Cut the eggplants in half lengthwise and score the surface of the cut sides with the point of a knife, cutting through the flesh to a depth of about 1/4 inch every inch or so, in a checkerboard pattern. (This facilitates seasoning and cooking.) Sprinkle with the oil, being especially generous on the cut sides, and the salt.

2. The grill must be very clean and very hot. Place the eggplant halves cut side down on the grill, cover with the lid, and cook for 5 minutes. Turn the eggplant halves over, cover again, and cook for 5 minutes on the other side. (If a grill is not available, cook the eggplant in a covered stainless steel or cast-iron skillet over very high heat for 5 minutes a side, until soft.) Arrange the eggplant on a platter, cut side up.

3. *For the dressing:* Mix together well the soy sauce, rice vinegar, sugar, and oil. Spoon over the eggplant and sprinkle with the chives. (This can be done 1 to 2 hours ahead of serving so the flavors have time to blend.)

4. Serve at room temperature.

YIELD: 6 SERVINGS

VEAL TENDRONS
AND TARRAGON SAUCE

TOTAL TIME:

1 HOUR AND

45 MINUTES

This dish can be made with or without cream. The richer version here contains a half cup of cream. Since the recipe serves six people, this amounts to only a little over a tablespoon of cream per person. The tarragon works particularly well in this combination. If fresh tarragon is unavailable, you can substitute dried tarragon.

The searing and browning of the veal create a crust of juices in the bottom of the cooking pan that lends taste to the sauce. Brown the meat at a temperature high enough so the juices crystallize into a dark-brown glaze but not so high that they burn. Except for the addition of cream, which should be made at serving time, the veal can be prepared ahead and refrigerated or frozen for later use.

1 *tablespoon vegetable oil*

1 *tablespoon unsalted butter*

1 *3½- to 4-pound veal breast, cut into ribs and each rib cut in half crosswise (there should be about 8 pieces)*

2 *onions (about 8 ounces), peeled and coarsely chopped*

1 *tablespoon all-purpose flour*

4 *cloves garlic, peeled, crushed, and coarsely chopped (about 1 tablespoon)*

2 *bay leaves and 5 to 6 sprigs thyme tied together to make an herb bouquet (see Note)*

1 *teaspoon salt*

½ *cup heavy cream*

1 *tablespoon fresh tarragon leaves or ½ teaspoon dried tarragon*

¼ *teaspoon freshly ground black pepper*

1. Heat the oil and butter in a sturdy enamel or cast-iron pan and, when hot, add half the veal ribs in one layer. Cook over high heat for about 10 minutes, turning to brown on all sides. Remove the browned ribs to a plate. Repeat with the remaining ribs, placing them on the plate after they are browned.

2. Drain off all but 1 tablespoon fat from the cooking pan and add the onions. Cook for 3 to 4 minutes, stirring constantly. The onions should be wilted and mixed with the solidified meat juices loosened through stirring. Add the flour and mix well. Add 1¼ cups water and bring to a boil, stirring well.

3. Return the meat to the pan and add the garlic, herb bouquet, and salt. Bring to a boil, cover, reduce the heat to very low, and cook slowly for 1 hour. By then the meat should be tender and there should be approximately 1¼ to 1½ cups of lightly thickened sauce.

4. Discard the herb bouquet and add the cream. Bring to a boil, stir in the tarragon and pepper, and serve.

NOTE: If fresh thyme is not available, substitute ½ teaspoon dried thyme and add the bay leaves and dried thyme to the pan in step 3.

YIELD: 6 SERVINGS

POTATO SAUTÉ À CRU

TOTAL TIME:
35 TO 40
MINUTES

These are the classic *pommes sautées* served in France not only with stew, but also with roast of veal, poultry, or even fish.

2½ *pounds potatoes, preferably Idaho*

¼ *cup peanut, corn, or canola oil*

1 *tablespoon unsalted butter*

⅛ *teaspoon salt*

2 *tablespoons chopped chives*

1. Peel the potatoes and cut them into very thin slices. Wash in cold water and, if not ready to cook them, cover with fresh cold water and set aside. The potatoes will not discolor if completely submerged in the water.

2. At cooking time, drain the potatoes well and pat them dry with paper towels. Heat the oil in one large pan (12 to 14 inches) or two smaller ones (so the potatoes have room to brown). When hot, add the potatoes and spread them out in the pan(s). Cover the pan(s) and cook over medium to high heat, turning the potatoes carefully every 4 to 5 minutes so they brown on all sides, for 20 to 25 minutes, until the potatoes are soft and golden brown.

3. Stir in the butter, salt, and chives, and serve immediately.

NOTE: Although the potatoes are best if cooked at the last moment, they can be partially cooked ahead: Sauté them as indicated in the recipe for 10 minutes, stirring every 3 to 4 minutes. Set aside in the skillet, uncovered. At mealtime, place the potatoes over high heat and cook 10 minutes more. (Restaurants use a similar procedure for cooking French fries, blanching them beforehand and frying them just before serving.)

YIELD: 6 SERVINGS

SALAD WITH GARLIC DRESSING

TOTAL TIME:
12 TO 15 MINUTES

If stored in a tightly sealed plastic bag, the cleaned and thoroughly dried salad greens will keep in the refrigerator for several days. The dressing can be made ahead and the recipe here doubled or tripled, with the excess stored in the refrigerator for use during the next several days.

1 *large, firm head (about 1 pound) curly chicory, escarole, or other salad green (about 6 packed cups)*

FOR THE DRESSING

2 *cloves garlic, peeled, crushed, and finely chopped (about 1 1/2 teaspoons)*

1 *tablespoon Dijon-style mustard*

1/4 *teaspoon salt*

1/4 *teaspoon freshly ground black pepper*

1 *tablespoon vinegar*

1/4 *cup vegetable or olive oil or a mixture of both*

1. Wash the salad greens thoroughly in a sink filled with cold water. Lift the greens from the water and spin dry in a salad spinner.

2. *For the dressing:* Stir together all the dressing ingredients in the bowl you will use for serving the salad.

3. At serving time, add the greens to the bowl and toss thoroughly with the dressing. Serve immediately.

YIELD: 6 SERVINGS

A CLASSIC EVERYDAY DISH-AND
GREAT AS LEFTOVERS, TOO

Pot-au-Feu

Vegetable and Vermicelli Soup
Beef, Turkey, and Mustard Salad

Pot-au-feu (pronounced poh-toe-FUH), the classic French boiled meat and vegetable dish, was the traditional winter Sunday lunch of my youth. Lunch was the biggest meal of the day, and dinner usually consisted of leftovers, along with fruit and cheese.

Originally part of the everyday cuisine of ordinary French people, the dish now is served in three-star restaurants in France as well as the smallest family inns and neighborhood bistros. But it has not, unfortunately, fared well in the fancier restaurants, which have attempted to refine it by shaping the vegetables and adding a much greater variety of meat. They have often made the dish so complicated and so contrived that it has lost its honest, straightforward character and forsaken its plebeian origins.

Versions of pot-au-feu—literally, "pot on the fire"—have been made in France since before the Middle Ages. It is classically made with tough but flavorful pieces of beef, such as the shin, brisket (top of the ribs), or, as in the following recipe, the shank.

continued

I like the shank because it is a moist, gelatinous cut of beef, yielding a strong, meaty-flavored stock while still remaining tender enough to eat. In addition, it is also one of the least expensive cuts on the market. I use a whole shank from a center cut that weighs about four pounds, about half of which is bone. If the recipe is made with sliced beef shank, the cooking time should be reduced by a half hour or so.

In some parts of France pot-au-feu is made somewhat more elegant with the addition of a stuffed hen, and in the south it is often flavored with mutton or veal knuckles. Yet it always contains beef or beef bones. Besides the beef shank, this recipe includes beef neck bones, which are usually meaty, and turkey, which is relatively inexpensive but flavorful.

For a more economical pot-au-feu, eliminate the shank and use more neck bones with the turkey. This version will produce less meat, but the broth and vegetables will be just as rich tasting.

Use a turkey leg, which is more moist than the breast, and some of a turkey carcass, which often is available inexpensively at most markets. Notice, however, that the turkey is removed before the pot-au-feu is finished cooking so it will not become too dry. The turkey meat is picked off the bones, which are returned to the cooking pot, and the meat is set aside in some broth until serving time.

This recipe calls for a great array of vegetables—carrots, celery, onions, potatoes, turnips, leeks, and cabbage. With one exception, the vegetables can be selected according to market availability and price. The leeks yield great flavor and are a must; unfortunately, they are sometimes very costly.

Traditionally, pot-au-feu is served with coarse salt on the side, cornichons (small gherkins in vinegar), hot mustard, and grated horseradish. The broth is served in large bowls set off to the side of each place setting, and the vegetables and beef are spooned from large trays onto the dinner plates. The meal can be finished with fruit, a custard, or ice cream. If wine is served, select a robust red.

While pot-au-feu does take a while to cook, it does not require a great amount of work. And the leftovers can be used to make a complete meal. First, I combine the broth with the cut-up leftover vegetables, bring it to a boil, and add pasta (in this case, vermicelli) to create an earthy, satisfying soup—which can be frozen for later consumption.

In addition, the leftover meat from the pot-au-feu can be transformed, as on page 238, into a spicy and invigorating beef and turkey salad, seasoned with mustard, onion, garlic, oil, and vinegar. Or sometimes the leftover meat is ground fine and made into meatballs, or sliced and sautéed with lots of onion and flavored with tomatoes for another classic French dish, beef mironton.

POT-AU-FEU

Some people may object to the stronger taste of cabbage or white turnips in this version of pot-au-feu. These can be eliminated or replaced with milder vegetables, like sweet potatoes, parsnips, or Napa cabbage.

Although not an absolute necessity (and not included in the recipe here), a burnt onion imparts a beautiful golden color to the stock and is a worthwhile addition to the dish. To prepare one, impale an unpeeled onion on a kitchen fork and hold it over the flame of a gas burner (or place it under the broiler) until burned on all sides. When cool enough to handle, stud with cloves and add to the stock with the salt, pepper, and bay leaves.

A very large stockpot (preferably stainless steel or enamel so it does not discolor) is essential for pot-au-feu. Mine holds about 15 to 20 quarts.

TOTAL TIME: 4 HOURS AND 15 MINUTES

1 *large beef shank (about 4 pounds)*

1½ *pounds beef neck bones (as meaty as possible)*

2 *turkey legs, and part of the carcass if available (about 3½ pounds)*

7 *small onions (about 14 ounces)*

12 *cloves*

4 *teaspoons salt*

1 *teaspoon freshly ground black pepper*

4 *bay leaves*

10 TO 12 *carrots (about 1 pound), peeled*

8 TO 10 *celery stalks (about 1 pound), outside ribs peeled with a vegetable peeler*

8 TO 10 *small potatoes (preferably red) of about equal size (about 1¼ pounds), peeled*

6 *small white turnips (about 1½ pounds), peeled*

3 TO 5 *leeks (about 1½ pounds), any damaged outer leaves removed and discarded, thoroughly cleaned*

1 *large head cabbage (about 1¾ pounds), cut into 8 wedges*

Cornichons, croutons or crusty bread, coarse salt, hot mustard, and grated horseradish, for garnish (see Note)

1. Place the beef shank, neck bones, and turkey in a large stockpot with 9 quarts cool tap water. (The longer time required to bring cool water to the boil helps draw more impurities from the meat. These will collect on the surface of the water in the form of a foam.) Bring to a boil over high heat (this may take as long as 45 minutes).

2. Peel the onions, and stud 1 with the cloves.

3. When the cooking liquid has come to a full boil, use a fine skimmer to remove any foam that has risen to the top and discard it. Continue boiling gently for about 20 minutes, removing any additional foam.

4. Add the salt, pepper, bay leaves, and the clove-studded onion. Partially cover the pot, leaving about a 1-inch opening for the steam to escape (this saves fuel and keeps the liquid from clouding), and cook gently for about 1 1/2 hours. (The seasonings are not added to the stock at the outset because they would get skimmed off along with the foam that rises to the surface early in the cooking.)

5. Remove the turkey, but continue cooking the beef. When the turkey is cool enough to handle, remove and discard the skin and pick the meat from the bones. Cover the turkey meat to prevent it from drying out and set it aside. Return the bones to the pot to continue cooking for 1 hour longer.

6. When the beef is completely cooked (it should be tender when pierced with a fork), remove it with a large skimmer and place it on a tray. With the skimmer, lift out and discard any particles or pieces of bone from the liquid to produce as clear a stock as possible. Using a ladle, skim as much fat as you can from the surface of the liquid.

7. When the beef is cool enough to handle, remove the meat from the bones and slice it and the reserved turkey meat into serving pieces. Place them in a large gratin dish with 2 to 3 cups of the stock, cover, and set aside to reheat at serving time.

8. About 45 minutes before serving, add all the vegetables, including the remaining onions, to the stock, bring to a boil (it will take 15 to 20 minutes), and boil gently for about 20 minutes.

9. With the large skimmer, transfer all the vegetables to a tray or large platter and cover to keep warm. Reheat the beef and turkey meat in the 2 to 3 cups of stock, either on top of the stove, in a conventional oven, or in a microwave oven.

10. Serve the stock in large bowls set next to the dinner plates, and bring the meat and vegetables to the table on trays or platters. Serve the stock with croutons or crusty bread, if desired, and pass around coarse salt, pickles, mustard, and/or horseradish to eat with the meat and vegetables.

NOTE: The cornichons can be replaced by regular sour pickles and the salt can be omitted. Toasted bread or croutons are often served with the broth, along with grated Swiss or Parmesan cheese, and sometimes the marrow from the bones is spread on toast or croutons and eaten with the broth.

YIELD: 6 SERVINGS, WITH ENOUGH LEFTOVERS FOR VEGE-TABLE AND VERMICELLI SOUP AND BEEF, TURKEY, AND MUSTARD SALAD

FROM THE LEFTOVERS

VEGETABLE AND VERMICELLI SOUP

Since this recipe is made, essentially, with leftovers from the Pot-au-Feu, your proportions may be slightly different. Increase or decrease the amount of pasta you add, based on the amount of stock and vegetables that remain. I used vermicelli, a very thin pasta, but you can use anything from macaroni to alphabet noodles if you prefer.

TOTAL TIME:
35 TO 40 MINUTES

3 *quarts stock from Pot-au-Feu (page 235)*
About 1 quart cut-up (1-inch pieces) leftover vegetables from Pot-au-Feu
4 *ounces (about 2 cups, loose) vermicelli, broken up (see above)*
Bread or toast, for garnish

1. Combine the stock and leftover vegetables in a pot and bring to a boil. Add the vermicelli and cook for about 8 to 10 minutes, until the pasta is just tender. Serve with bread or toast.

YIELD: 6 SERVINGS

BEEF, TURKEY, AND MUSTARD SALAD

TOTAL TIME:
ABOUT 15
MINUTES You may have more or less leftover meat from the pot-au-feu. Scale down or increase the proportions of other ingredients accordingly.

FOR THE DRESSING

2 *cloves garlic, crushed and chopped fine (about 1 teaspoon)*
2 *tablespoons Dijon-style mustard*
2 *tablespoons red wine vinegar*
1/4 *cup canola oil*
1/2 *teaspoon freshly ground black pepper*
1/4 *teaspoon salt*

3 1/2 *cups cut-up (1-inch pieces) leftover meat from Pot-au-Feu (page 235)*
3/4 *cup coarsely chopped onion*
3 *scallions, cleaned and finely minced (about 1/3 cup)*
1/4 *cup coarsely chopped parsley*

Lettuce leaves, for garnish

1. Combine the dressing ingredients together in a large serving bowl. Add the meat, onion, scallions, and parsley, and toss to mix. Serve at room temperature on lettuce leaves.

YIELD: 6 SERVINGS

COMFORT FOOD:
MEAT AND POTATOES

Carrot and Scallion Salad
Salisbury "Steaks" with Vegetable Sauce
Garlic Mashed Potatoes

Everyone likes mashed potatoes. They are "comfort food," pleasing to children and adults alike, haute cuisine buffs as well as fast food addicts. And nothing complements mashed potatoes like gravy—be it the natural juices from a veal roast, thickened pan drippings from a roast turkey, or, as in this menu, vegetable sauce from around a meat loaf.

The Garlic Mashed Potatoes here remind me of my beloved godmother and aunt, who would always add a few cloves of garlic to the potato cooking water. The delicate taste of garlic this imparted to the dish is forever associated in my mind with the summer vacations of my youth along the chalky banks of the Rhône river.

Instead of making the meat loaf in the traditional way by molding it in a loaf pan, I form it here into patties or "steaks"—hence the name, Salisbury steaks—for Dr. James H. Salisbury, whose prescription for good health in the late 1800s was to eat "muscle pulp of lean beef made into cakes and broiled."

continued

In this recipe, far more healthful by today's standards and more economical, only half of the steak mixture is meat; the remainder is made up of chopped vegetables (onion, celery, and garlic), unpeeled apple cubes, and fresh bread crumbs. Extended in this way, the one and a half pounds of ground beef yields six large patties, which cook in about thirty minutes. The same mixture placed in a large loaf pan will take forty-five minutes to an hour (until the internal temperature reaches 145 to 150 degrees) to cook.

The vegetable sauce served with the steaks is made independently and partially cooked on top of the stove, then finished in the oven with the patties, after the fat that has accumulated around them in the first twenty minutes of cooking is drained away. This second cooking of the sauce in the oven intensifies its taste and flavors the meat. The crunchy, invigorating Carrot and Scallion Salad makes a great starter and can be prepared quickly since the carrots can be grated in a few seconds in a food processor.

A robust red wine, perhaps a Zinfandel or Beaujolais, goes perfectly with this earthy, simple, satisfying menu, which is best finished with a dessert featuring fresh fruit.

CARROT AND SCALLION SALAD

Leftover salad is excellent in sandwiches with leftover Salisbury steak or other cold cuts.

TOTAL TIME: 15 MINUTES

FOR THE DRESSING

1 teaspoon salt

1 teaspoon freshly ground black pepper

$^1/_4$ teaspoon Tabasco sauce

2 tablespoons red wine vinegar

$^1/_3$ cup safflower or canola oil

1 pound carrots (about 8 to 10), peeled and shredded by hand or in a food processor (about 4 cups)

About 12 scallions, dark green leaf tips and damaged leaves removed and discarded, cut crosswise into $^1/_4$-inch slices (2 cups)

2 TO 3 cloves garlic, peeled, crushed, and very finely chopped (about 1 teaspoon)

$^1/_2$ cup coarsely chopped parsley

8 TO 10 lettuce leaves, for garnish

1. *For the dressing:* Combine the salt, pepper, Tabasco, vinegar, and oil in a bowl.

2. Add the shredded carrots, scallions, and garlic to the dressing, and mix well. Stir in the parsley.

3. Clean the lettuce leaves, removing the center rib from each if it is thick and tough, and arrange the leaves on individual serving plates. Arrange spoonfuls of the salad on top of the lettuce leaves and serve with crunchy bread.

NOTE: This can be prepared ahead and refrigerated until serving time.

YIELD: 6 SERVINGS

SALISBURY "STEAKS" WITH VEGETABLE SAUCE

TOTAL TIME:
1 HOUR

I make a pound and a half of ground beef go far by extending it with the addition of chopped vegetables, apples, and fresh bread crumbs. Salisbury steak leftovers are very good cold. Cut the steaks, or larger loaf, into thin slices and serve like a pâté, or use as a sandwich filling with a hot mustard to enhance the mildly sweet taste of the diced apple in the mixture.

half recipe:

FOR THE MEAT MIXTURE

1/2 3 tablespoons corn or canola oil

3/4 1½ cups chopped onion

3/4 1½ cups minced celery

1 2 apples (about 1 pound; Rome Beauties are a good choice)

3/4 lb 1½ pounds ground beef

1 2 large eggs

1/2 tsp 2 TO 3 cloves garlic, peeled, crushed, and finely chopped (about 1 teaspoon)

1/4 1 teaspoon salt

1/4 ½ teaspoon freshly ground pepper

2 2 TO 3 slices firm, fresh bread (to make 1½ cups fresh bread crumbs) (see Special Tip)

FOR THE SAUCE

1 2 medium-size carrots, peeled

1/2 1 medium-size to large onion, peeled

1/2 1 tablespoon dark soy sauce

1/4 ¼ teaspoon freshly ground black pepper

1 1½ tablespoons tomato paste

1/4 ¼ teaspoon Tabasco sauce

1/4 ½ teaspoon salt

1. *For the meat mixture:* Heat the oil in a saucepan. When hot, add the onion and celery and cook for 4 to 5 minutes over medium heat, until the vegetables are softened slightly.

2. Meanwhile, core but do not peel the apples. Cut them into ½-inch pieces. (You should have about 2 cups.) Add to the onion and celery mixture and set aside.

3. Place the meat in a large bowl. Add the onion-celery-apple mixture to it along with the eggs, garlic, salt, and pepper, and mix well.

4. Tear the slices of bread into large pieces and place in the bowl of a food processor. Process until crumbed. You should have 1 ½ cups. (Fresh bread crumbs are best for this recipe; if substituting dry crumbs, use only ¾ cup.) Add to the meat mixture and mix well to incorporate.

5. Dampen your hands with water and form the mixture into 6 large patties (each weighing approximately ½ pound). Arrange in a large roasting pan so there is a little space between the "steaks," and bake in a preheated 400-degree oven for 20 minutes.

6. *Meanwhile, for the sauce:* Coarsely chop the peeled carrots and onion in a food processor or by hand. (You should have about 2 cups total.) Place in a saucepan with 2 cups water, the soy sauce, pepper, tomato paste, Tabasco, and salt. Bring to a boil, reduce the heat, and boil gently for 5 minutes.

7. When the steaks have cooked for 20 minutes, remove them from the oven. They will probably stick to the bottom of the pan so you can easily incline the pan and pour off most of the accumulated fat around them. Spoon the sauce over and around the steaks and return them to the oven for 10 minutes. Serve warm.

YIELD: 6 SERVINGS

*S*PECIAL TIP: *One standard slice of fresh bread processed in a food processor will yield ½ to ¾ cup of fresh bread crumbs. If dried, that same slice of bread will yield approximately 3 to 4 tablespoons of dried bread crumbs. Be sure to take this into account when you are using bread crumbs in a recipe; use about half the amount of dried crumbs as a replacement for fresh crumbs.*

GARLIC MASHED POTATOES

TOTAL TIME:
40 TO 45
MINUTES

The potatoes are cooked until tender, drained, and then mashed immediately. It is important that they be mashed while still hot, directly after draining; if left to cool, they tend to get stringy. If the potatoes are put through a food mill, as they are here, the garlic doesn't even have to be peeled, since the skin will not go through the mill. If, however, you plan to mash the potatoes by hand, peel the cloves before adding them to the cooking water.

Leftover potatoes can be reheated in a microwave oven, fried in a skillet, or added to soup as a flavor enhancer and thickener.

2 *pounds potatoes*

4 *large cloves garlic*

1¼ *teaspoons salt*

2 *tablespoons butter*

1 *cup milk (see Note)*

⅛ *teaspoon freshly ground black pepper*

1. Peel the potatoes, wash them under cold water, and cut into large chunks (2 to 2½-inch pieces). Place in a pot with water to cover and add the garlic and 1 teaspoon of the salt. Bring to a boil, reduce the heat, and boil gently until the potatoes are tender, about 22 to 25 minutes.

2. Pour directly into a food mill, first placing a pot underneath to catch the cooking liquid, which can be retained for use in stocks, soups, or bread. Then push the potatoes through the food mill into a bowl. Add the butter and mix in thoroughly, then add the milk, mixing again until incorporated. Add the remaining ¼ teaspoon salt and the pepper and stir in. Serve with the Salisbury steaks, spooning some of the vegetable sauce over the potatoes.

NOTE: If desired, a little of the potato cooking liquid can be added to the potatoes as a flavorful replacement for some of the milk, and any remaining cooking liquid can be reserved for use in soups, in bread dough, or as a replacement for water or stock in some sauces.

YIELD: 6 SERVINGS

DOWN-HOME FAVORITES IN ELEGANT DRESS

Grits and Cheese Soufflé
Braised Pork and Cabbage

This menu features heart-warming dishes that are copious and earthy, yet a bit elegant too. Start the pork early in the day if you plan to serve it for dinner; it doesn't involve much work, but it must cook very slowly for a long time to be flavorful. It can be made ahead completely and reheated, or it can be partially cooked and then finished at serving time for a fresher taste. The meat is first rubbed with a combination of herbs and spices—oregano, cumin, allspice, and cayenne—and then cooked with Savoy cabbage seasoned with sugar and vinegar to achieve a sweet-sour flavor.

The Grits and Cheese Soufflé makes a terrific first course, but it also could be served, with a salad, as a main course for a brunch or light supper. It requires a little preparation, although some of this can be done ahead. The grits, made of hulled and ground corn and also known as hominy grits or white hominy, can be cooked ahead with the scallions and milk.

A salad would be welcome here, as well as a fruity, robust wine; a Sicilian red, like a Corvo, is a good choice and such wines are often very well priced.

GRITS AND CHEESE SOUFFLÉ

TOTAL TIME:
40 MINUTES

The soufflé can be baked in a soufflé mold, but when cooked in a gratin dish it is crustier, easy to serve, and beautiful to look at. It also can be reheated and served as a pudding.

6 *scallions, damaged and wilted outer leaves removed, cut into ¹/₄-inch pieces (about ³/₄ cup)*

2¹/₂ *cups whole or skim milk*

¹/₂ *teaspoon salt*

¹/₄ *teaspoon freshly ground black pepper*

¹/₄ *cup grits (white hominy)*

4 *ounces Cheddar cheese, 1 slice reserved to cut into diamonds or strips to decorate the top of the soufflé and the remainder grated (1¹/₄ cups)*

5 *large eggs, separated*

1. Butter a 6-cup gratin dish and set it aside.

2. Place the scallions, milk, salt, and pepper in a saucepan and bring to a boil over medium to high heat. Stir in the grits and return the mixture to a boil. Reduce the heat and boil gently for 12 to 15 minutes, stirring occasionally, until thickened and cooked.

3. Stir in the grated cheese, then immediately mix in the egg yolks. Remove the pan from the heat. The recipe can be prepared to this point several hours ahead. If the grits are made ahead, however, be sure to thin the mixture with a little water before completing the recipe, as grits tend to thicken as they cool.

4. About half an hour before serving time, beat the egg whites in a large bowl until firm and fold them into the grits mixture with a rubber spatula. Pour the mixture into the buttered gratin dish and decorate with diamonds or strips cut from the reserved slice of cheese.

5. Place the soufflé in the center of a preheated 350-degree oven and bake for about 20 minutes, until the soufflé is just set and puffy. Serve immediately. (The soufflé will deflate quickly, so eat it as soon as it emerges from the oven. Or serve lukewarm; it is still good.)

YIELD: 6 SERVINGS

SPECIAL TIP   GRITS BREAKFAST SOUPS: *For a hearty breakfast soup, follow the instructions in Step 2 of the soufflé recipe, cooking the grits in the milk, scallions, salt, and pepper. Serve this savory mixture as a warm beginning to a cold, wintry day.*

BRAISED PORK AND CABBAGE

Make the braised pork with a piece of pork butt or shoulder or a loin tip roast, so named because it comes from the end of the loin, which is attached to the shoulder. These cuts are relatively inexpensive and will produce a moist and delicious result.

TOTAL TIME: 3 HOURS AND 45 MINUTES

2   teaspoons salt

2   teaspoons dried oregano

1   teaspoon cumin powder

1/2   teaspoon allspice powder

1/4   teaspoon cayenne pepper

1   4-pound pork roast (loin tip, shoulder, or pork butt)

1   tablespoon virgin olive oil

1   large or 2 medium-size heads Savoy cabbage (about 2 1/2 pounds), leaves cut into 2-inch pieces and core cut into 1/2-inch pieces

2   large onions (about 1 pound), peeled and sliced

1   tablespoon sugar

1/2   cup cider vinegar

1   tablespoon dark soy sauce

1. Mix together the salt, oregano, cumin, allspice, and cayenne, and rub the mixture all over the roast.

2. Heat the olive oil in a sturdy Dutch oven or large casserole. When hot, add the roast and brown it over medium to high heat for about 30 minutes, turning occasionally, until well browned on all sides. Cover tightly with a lid, place in a preheated 325-degree oven, and cook for 1 hour.

3. Remove the roast from the oven and transfer it to a platter. Combine the cabbage, onions, sugar, vinegar, and soy sauce in the Dutch oven. Position the roast on top of the cabbage mixture, cover tightly, and return the pot to the oven for another 2 hours. (The roast should have released a lot of juice and be fork tender.)

4. Slice the roast and serve it with the cabbage and the natural juices that have accumulated in the pot.

YIELD: 6 SERVINGS

INDEX

Page numbers in **bold type** refer to recipes.

warm vegetable salad, 83, **84–85**
Catfish:
with croutons and nuts, 215–216, **218–219**
seafood gumbo, 191–192, **193–194**
Cauliflower:
and crumbs, 34, **37**
grand aïoli, 75–76, **77–79**
pickled vegetables Gerry, 70, **73**
soup, 221, **222**
vegetable and pasta stew, 145, **148–149**
warm vegetable salad, 83, **84–85**
Cayettes with spinach, 15–16, **18–19**
Celery:
and apple salad, 198, **199**
chicken hearts and gizzards soup, 215, **216–217**
grand aïoli, 75–76, **77–79**
pot-au-feu, 233–234, **235–237**
warm vegetable salad, 83, **84–85**
Celery cabbage salad, 61, **64**
Chablis, 178
Chamart, 210
Champvallon, lamb chops, 139, **142–143**
Chard, Swiss:
and black-eyed peas ragout, 197–199, **200–201**
cayettes with, 15–16, **18–19**
gratin, 122, **126**
Chardonnay, 128
Chateau Ste. Michelle, 116
Cheddar cheese:
fiery chili with red beans, **177–179**
fromage fort, 163, **165**
and grits soufflé, 245, **246–247**
macaroni Beaucaire, 83, **86–87**
Cheese:
cream, and mint, guava with, **53**
fromage fort, 163, **165**
pasta shells with ricotta filling, 95, **98–99**
see also specific cheeses
Cheese, mozzarella:
fromage fort, 163, **165**
pissaladière baguettes, 151, **153**
and tomato salad, 28, **29**
Cheese, Parmesan:
gratin of butternut squash, 183–184, **186**
gratin of eggs and spinach, 55, **56–57**
herb-stuffed zucchini boats, 89, **92–93**

macaroni Beaucaire, 83, **86–87**
pasta shells with ricotta filling, 95, **98–99**
spaghetti with basil pesto, 89, **90–91**
vegetable and pasta stew, 145, **148–149**
zucchini-tomato gratin, 135, **137–138**
Cheese, Swiss:
fromage fort, 163, **165**
macaroni Beaucaire, 83, **86–87**
pissaladière baguettes, 151, **153**
Swiss chard gratin, 122, **126**
Cherry tomatoes:
pissaladière baguettes, 151, **153**
sautéed soy chicken, 209, **213–214**
Chianti, 221
Chicken:
baked, with herb crumbs, 107, **108–109**
boning of, 33–34, 35
crackling, 34
diable, 34, **35–36**
fricassee, lentil and, 34, **38–39**
grand aïoli, 75–76, **77–79**
hearts and gizzards soup, 215, **216–217**
sautéed soy, 209, **213–214**
skin, 34
stuffing, tomatoes with, 108, **112–113**
sweet and spicy curried, 27, **30–31**
Chicken livers, 34
cayettes with spinach, 15–16, **18–19**
hors d'oeuvre, **196**
in salad, 192, **195–196**
Chicken stock, 34, **108**
cauliflower soup, 221, **222**
garlic soup, **16–17**
hot or cold leek soup, 115, **116–117**
pumpkin and pastina soup, 203, **205**
rice with onions, **26**
zucchini-yogurt soup, 95, **96–97**
Chick peas, in grand aïoli, 75–76, **77–79**
Chicory salad with garlic dressing, 226, **231**
Chilean wines, 102
Chili with red beans, fiery, **177–179**
freezing of, 179
Chinese lettuce salad, 61, **64**
Chocolate sauce, for choux à la crème, 56, **59–60**

Chops:
lamb, Champvallon, 139, **142–143**
pork, grilled thyme, 136, **138**
Choux à la crème, 56, **59–60**
Chuck, beef:
fiery chili with red beans, **177–179**
spicy grilled beef roast, 122, **125**
Cider, 204
cozy, 198, **202**
Classic everyday dish—and great as leftovers, too (menu), 233–238
Codfish:
brandade de morue au gratin, 151–152, **154–155**
grand aïoli, 75–76, **77–79**
with olives, 102, **104**
and pasta with wine sauce, 164, **166–167**
seafood gumbo, 191–192, **193–194**
Cold or hot leek soup, 115, **116–117**
Cold weather warm-up (menu), 177–181
Cold zucchini terrine, **139–141**
Collard greens and black-eyed peas ragout, 197–199, **200–201**
Comfort food: meat and potatoes (menu), 239–244
Comforting food for a cold winter day (menu), 203–207
Compote, rhubarb, with sour cream, 107–108, **111**
Connecticut wines, 210
Cookies, with rhubarb compote with sour cream, 107–108, **111**
Corn:
off the cob, 170, **172**
salad, 145, **147**
tempura, 135, **136–137**
Cornichons, in pot-au-feu, 233–234, **235–237**
Corvo, 245
Côtes de Provence, 84, 122
Coupe, strawberry and orange, 95, **100**
Cozy cider, 198, **202**
Crackers, in guava with cream cheese and mint, **53**
Crackling:
chicken, 34
lentil and chicken fricassee, 34, **38–39**
turkey, escarole salad with, **8–9**
Cranberry:
kisel, 184, **187**
relish, **187**

About the Author

JACQUES PEPIN is one of the country's foremost cooking teachers. A columnist for *The New York Times,* he is also dean of studies at the French Culinary Institute in New York and an instructor at Boston University. He is the author of *The Short-Cut Cook, The Art of Cooking,* Volumes I and II, *Everyday Cooking with Jacques Pépin, La Technique,* and *La Méthode,* and hosts the television series *Today's Gourmet* on national PBS television. Pépin lives in Connecticut with his wife and daughter.